Math in Focus

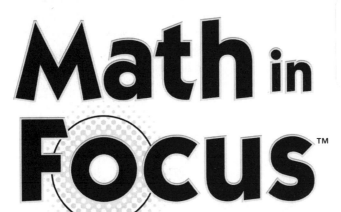

Singapore Math
by Marshall Cavendish

Extra Practice
1B

Author
Meena Newaskar

Marshall Cavendish
Education

GREAT SOURCE
HOUGHTON MIFFLIN HARCOURT
Supplemental Publishers

© 2009 Marshall Cavendish International (Singapore) Private Limited

Published by Marshall Cavendish Education
An imprint of Marshall Cavendish International (Singapore) Private Limited
Times Centre, 1 New Industrial Road, Singapore 536196
Customer Service Hotline: (65) 6411 0820
E-mail: tmesales@sg.marshallcavendish.com
Website: www.marshallcavendish.com/education

Distributed by
Great Source
A division of Houghton Mifflin Harcourt Publishing Company
181 Ballardvale Street
P.O. Box 7050
Wilmington, MA 01887-7050
Tel: 1-800-289-4490
Website: www.greatsource.com

First published 2009
Reprinted 2010 (twice), 2011

Marshall Cavendish and *Math in Focus*™ are trademarks of Times Publishing Limited.

Great Source ® is a registered trademark of Houghton Mifflin Harcourt Publishing Company.

Math in Focus Extra Practice 1B
ISBN 978-0-669-01568-3

Printed in United States of America

4 5 6 7 8   1897   16 15 14 13 12 11
4500279300   B C D E

Contents

Addition and Subtraction to 40

Mental Math Strategies

Calendar and Time

CHAPTER 19 Money

Introducing

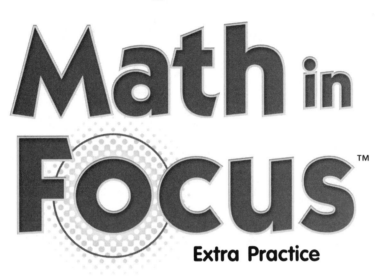

Math in Focus™

Extra Practice

Extra Practice 1A and *1B*, written to complement *Math in Focus™: Singapore Math by Marshall Cavendish* Grade 1, offer further practice very similar to the Practice exercises in the Student Books and Workbooks for on-level students.

Extra Practice provides ample questions to reinforce all the concepts taught, and includes challenging questions in the Put on Your Thinking Cap! pages. These pages provide extra non-routine problem-solving opportunities, strengthening critical thinking skills.

Extra Practice is an excellent option for homework, or may be used in class or after school. It is intended for students who simply need more practice to become confident, or secure students who are aiming for excellence.

BLANK

Name: _____   Date: _____

CHAPTER 10 Weight

Lesson 1   Comparing Things

Which is heavier?
Circle the answer.

1.

feather

apple

2.

book

envelope

3.

balloon

soccer ball

Which is lighter?
Circle the answer.

4.

butterfly

bird

5.

puppy

bear

6.

tree

leaf

7. Check (✓) the heavier fruit.

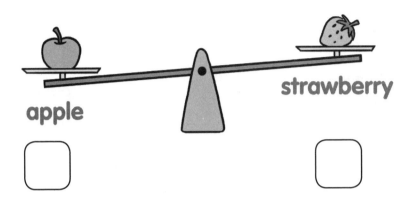

apple

strawberry

☐ ☐

8. Check (✓) the lighter animal.

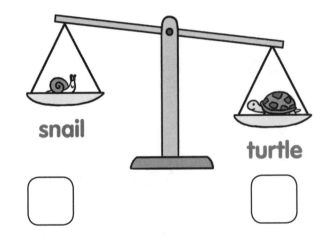

snail

turtle

☐ ☐

Fill in the blanks with *heavier than, lighter than,* or *as heavy as.*

9.

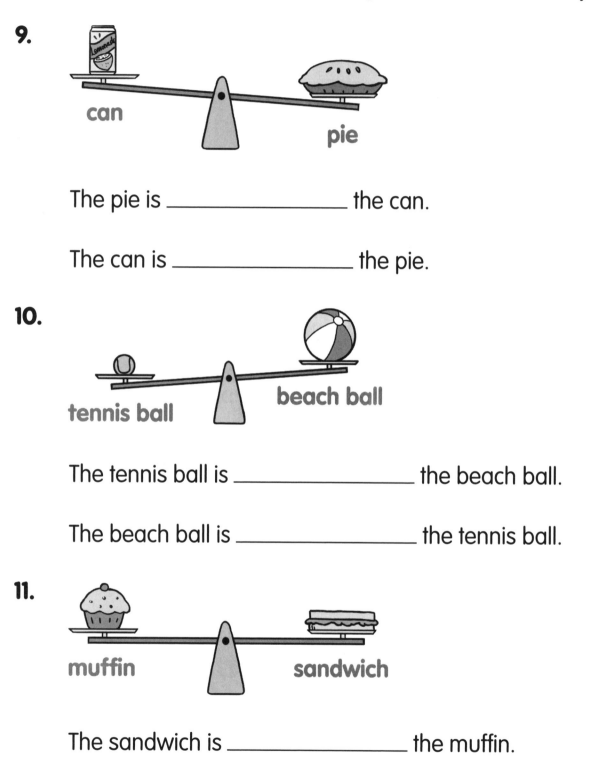

The pie is _____ the can.

The can is _____ the pie.

10.

The tennis ball is _____ the beach ball.

The beach ball is _____ the tennis ball.

11.

The sandwich is _____ the muffin.

● **Fill in the blanks.**

12.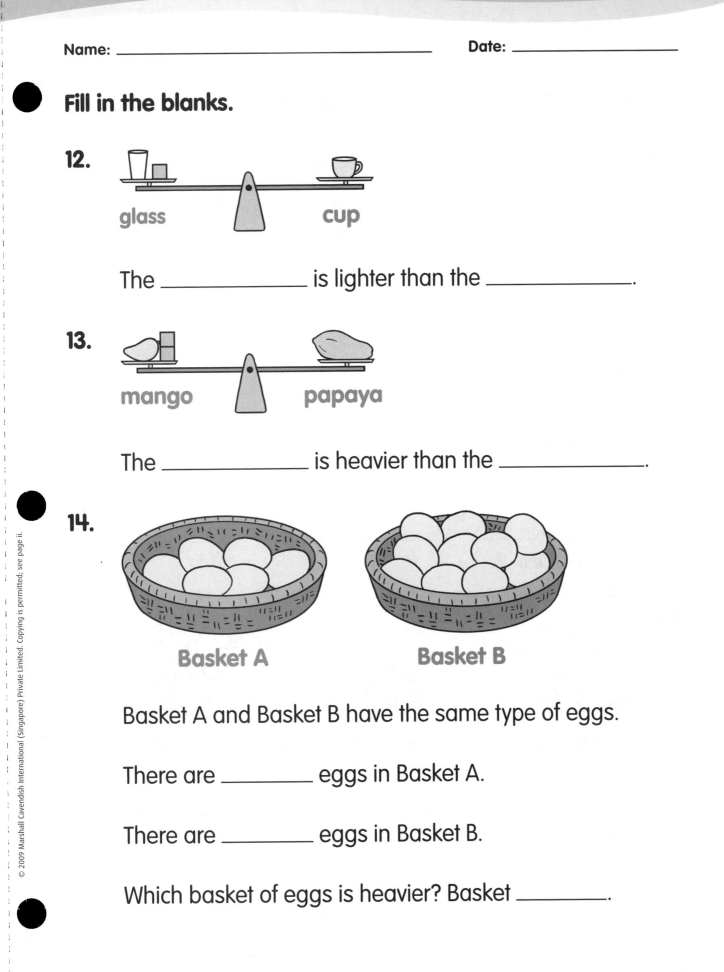

glass   cup

The _____ is lighter than the _____.

13.

mango   papaya

The _____ is heavier than the _____.

● 14.

Basket A   **Basket B**

Basket A and Basket B have the same type of eggs.

There are _____ eggs in Basket A.

There are _____ eggs in Basket B.

Which basket of eggs is heavier? Basket _____.

Order the animals from heaviest to lightest.

15.

chick   cow   sheep

_____   _____   _____
heaviest

16.

worm   fish   ant

_____   _____   _____
heaviest

17.

mouse   ladybug   squirrel

_____   _____   _____
heaviest

Lesson 2 Finding the Weight of Things

Fill in the blanks.

1.

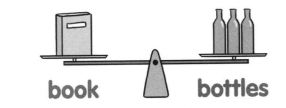

The weight of the book is about _____ bottles.

2.

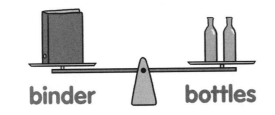

The weight of the binder is about _____ bottles.

3.

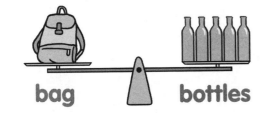

The weight of the bag is about _____ bottles.

Fill in the blanks.

4.

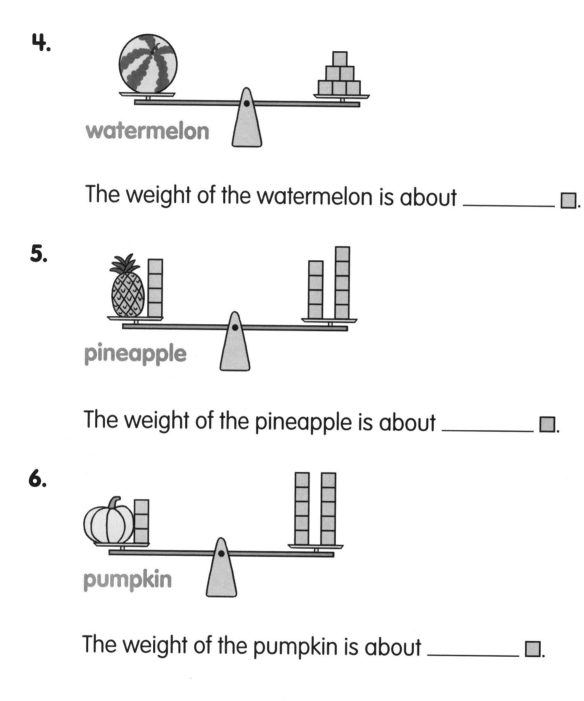

watermelon

The weight of the watermelon is about _____ □.

5.

pineapple

The weight of the pineapple is about _____ □.

6.

pumpkin

The weight of the pumpkin is about _____ □.

Name: _____   **Date:** _____

Look at the pictures.
Then fill in the blanks.

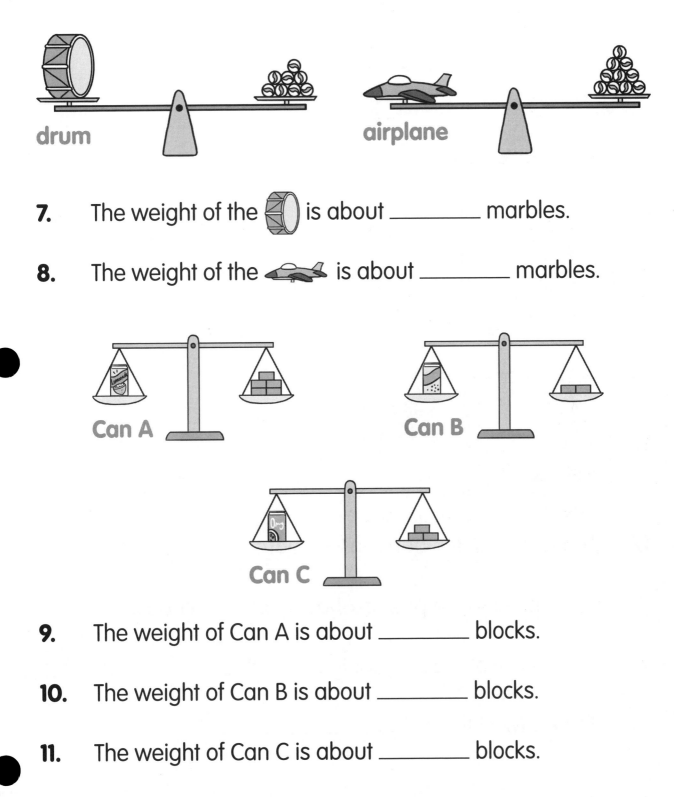

drum   airplane

7.   The weight of the ⬤ is about _____ marbles.

8.   The weight of the ✈ is about _____ marbles.

Can A   Can B

Can C

9.   The weight of Can A is about _____ blocks.

10.   The weight of Can B is about _____ blocks.

11.   The weight of Can C is about _____ blocks.

**Look at the pictures.
Then fill in the blanks.**

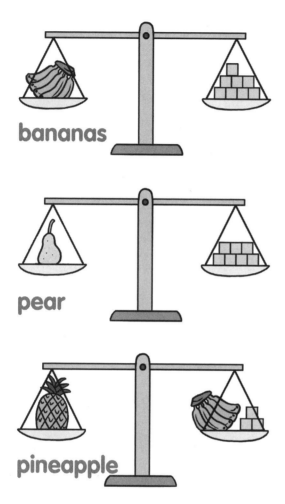

bananas

pear

pineapple

12. The weight of the bananas is about _____ cubes.

13. The weight of the pear is about _____ cubes.

14. The weight of the pineapple is about _____ cubes.

15. The heaviest fruit is the _____.

Lesson 3 Finding Weight in Units

Fill in the blanks.

1 ☐ stands for 1 unit.

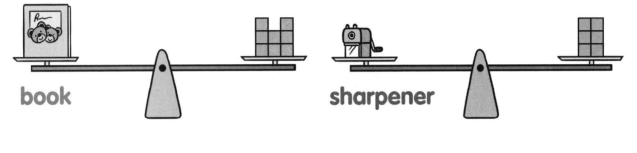

1.   The weight of the book is _____ units.

2.   The weight of the sharpener is _____ units.

1 ⊘ stands for 1 unit.

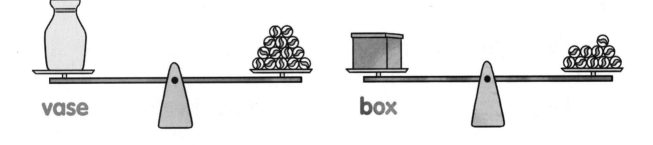

3.   The weight of the vase is _____ units.

4.   The weight of the box is _____ units.

Fill in the blanks.

1 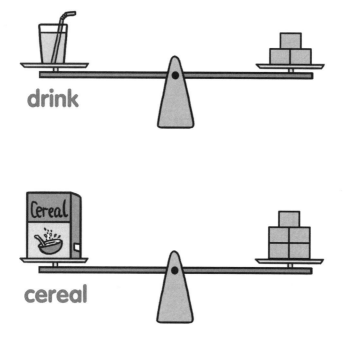 stands for 1 unit.

drink

cereal

5. The weight of the drink is _____ units.

6. The weight of the box of cereal is _____ units.

7. The _____ is heavier than the drink.

8. The drink is lighter than the box of _____.

Fill in the blanks.

1 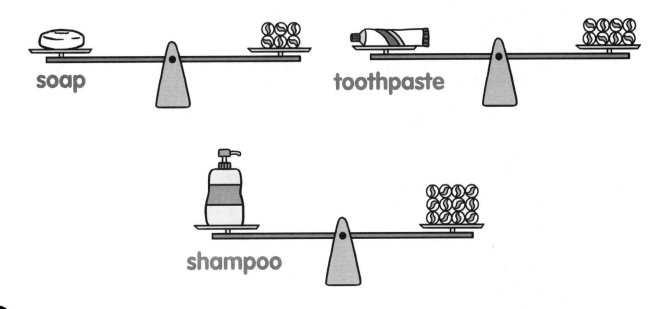 stands for 1 unit.

soap

toothpaste

shampoo

9. The weight of the soap is _____ units.

10. The weight of the toothpaste is _____ units.

11. The weight of the shampoo is _____ units.

12. The total weight of the soap and the toothpaste is

_____ units.

Fill in the blanks.

1 ☐ stands for 1 unit.

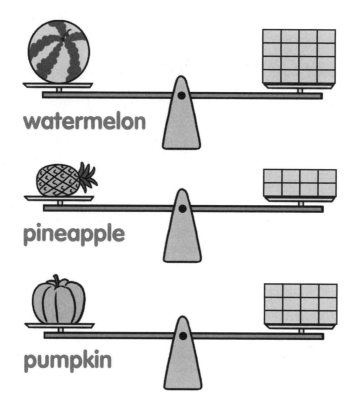

13. The weight of the watermelon is _____ units.

14. The weight of the pineapple is _____ units.

15. The weight of the pumpkin is _____ units.

16. Which is the lightest? _____

17. Which is the heaviest? _____

Name: _____ Date: _____

Fill in the blanks.

1 ⬤ stands for 1 unit.

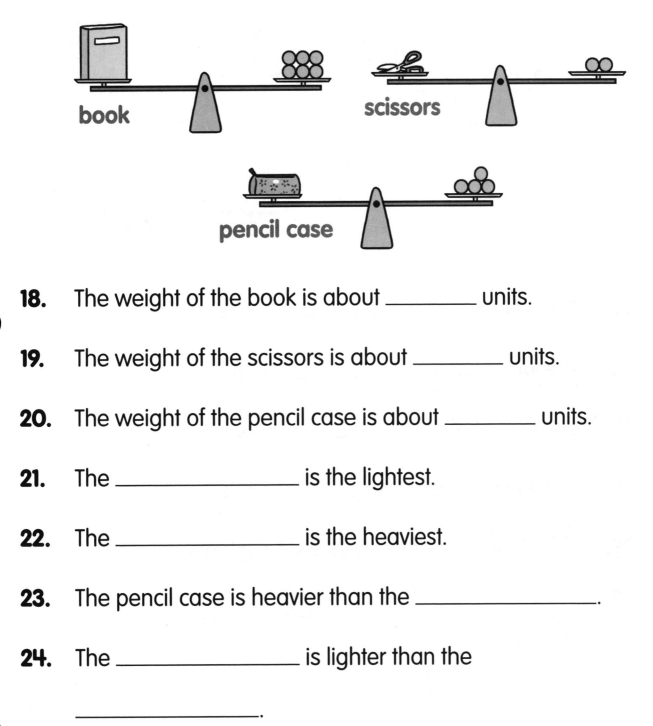

18. The weight of the book is about _____ units.

19. The weight of the scissors is about _____ units.

20. The weight of the pencil case is about _____ units.

21. The _____ is the lightest.

22. The _____ is the heaviest.

23. The pencil case is heavier than the _____.

24. The _____ is lighter than the

_____.

Fill in the blanks.

1 ▢ stands for 1 unit.

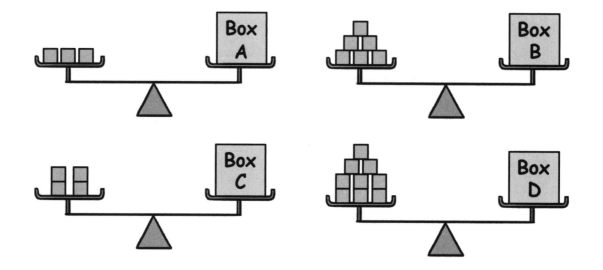

25. The weight of Box A is _____ units.

26. The weight of Box B is _____ units.

27. The weight of Box C is _____ units.

28. The weight of Box D is _____ units.

29. Order the boxes from heaviest to lightest.

_____, _____, _____, _____

heaviest

Put on Your Thinking Cap!

Look at the pictures.
Then fill in the blanks.

The weight of 1 snail is 6 units.

= 6 units

The weight of 1 turtle and 1 snail is 16 units.

+ = 16 units

The weight of 1 turtle and 1 caterpillar is 13 units.

 = 13 units

1.   The weight of 1 snail is _____ units.

2.   The weight of 1 turtle is _____ units.

3.   The weight of 1 caterpillar is _____ units.

Look at the pictures.
Then answer the questions.

kitten   hamster

puppy   kitten

4. Which is the heaviest? _____

5. Which is the lightest? _____

CHAPTER 11 Picture Graphs and Bar Graphs

Lesson 1   Simple Picture Graphs

Look at the picture graph.
Then fill in the blanks.

The graph shows the number of books read by 3 children in a week.

Number of Books Read

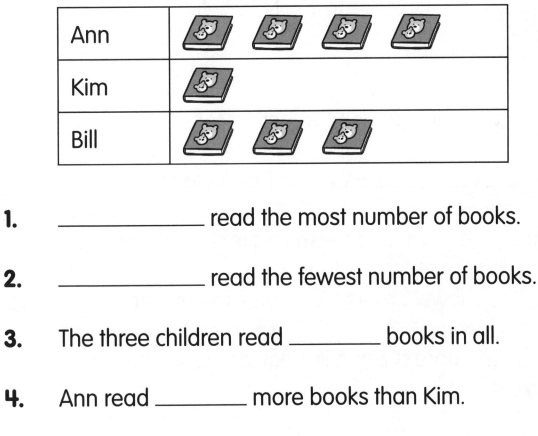

1. _____ read the most number of books.

2. _____ read the fewest number of books.

3. The three children read _____ books in all.

4. Ann read _____ more books than Kim.

Look at the picture graph.
Then fill in the blanks.

The graph shows the favorite stickers of some children.

Favorite Stickers

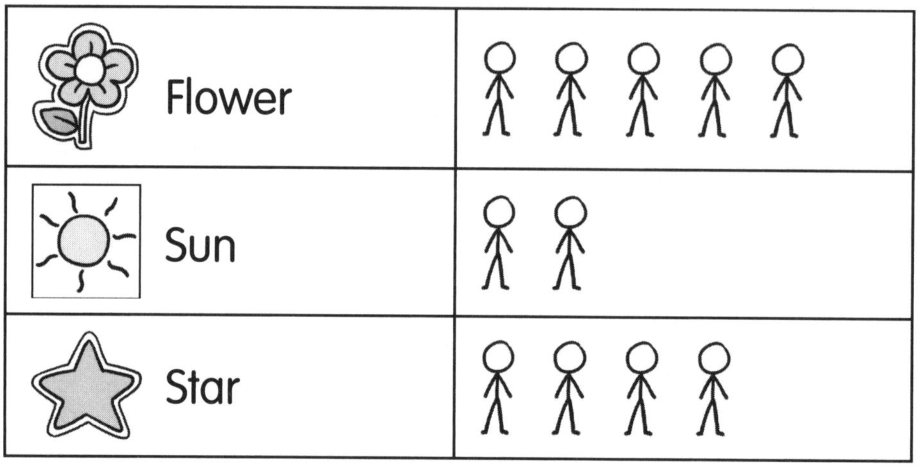

Flower	𝔸 𝔸 𝔸 𝔸 𝔸
Sun	𝔸 𝔸
Star	𝔸 𝔸 𝔸 𝔸

5. _____ children like flower stickers.

6. The _____ is the least popular sticker.

7. The _____ is the most popular sticker.

8. _____ fewer children like sun stickers than star stickers.

9. _____ more children like flower stickers than sun stickers.

Name: _____ Date: _____

Look at the picture graph.
Then fill in the blanks.

The graph shows the favorite sea animals of some children.

Favorite Sea Animals

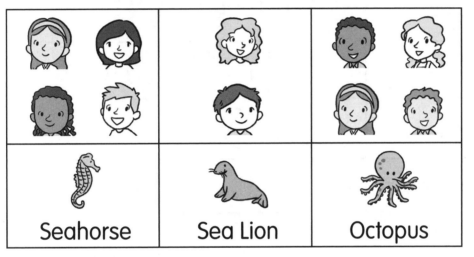

Seahorse	Sea Lion	Octopus

10. How many children like the octopus? _____

11. How many more children like the seahorse than

    the sea lion? _____

12. Circle the sea animals that are liked by an equal number
    of children.

Look at the picture graph.
Then fill in the blanks.

The graph shows the fruits that Kimberly bought.

Fruits Kimberly Bought

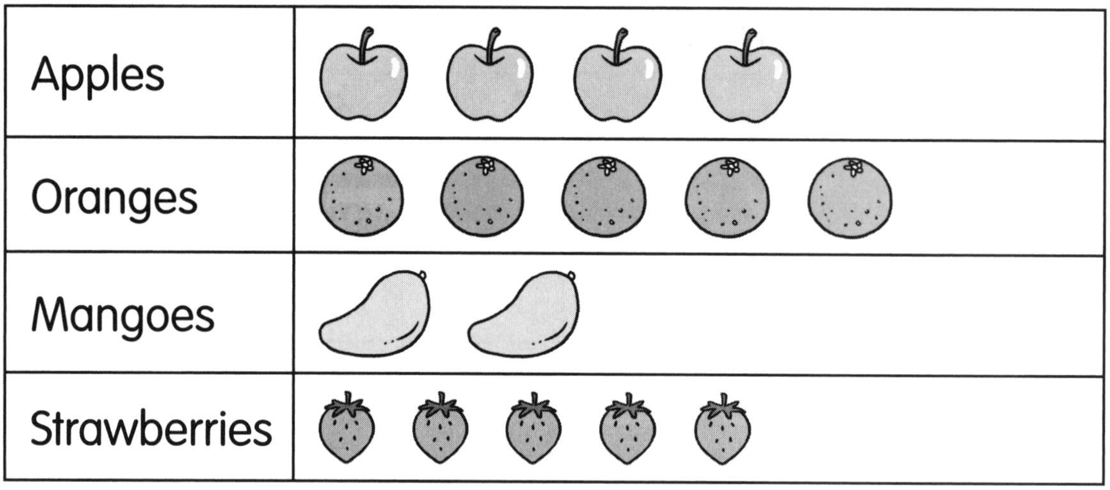

Apples	🍎 🍎 🍎 🍎
Oranges	🍊 🍊 🍊 🍊 🍊
Mangoes	🥭 🥭
Strawberries	🍓 🍓 🍓 🍓 🍓

13. The number of _____ is the least.

14. How many more oranges than mangoes did

Kimberly buy? _____

15. How many fewer apples than strawberries did

Kimberly buy? _____

16. Kimberly bought an equal number of oranges

and _____.

17. Kimberly bought _____ fruits in all.

● Lesson 2   More Picture Graphs

Look at the picture graph.
Then fill in the blanks.

The graph shows the points scored by 3 boys in a game.

Points Scored in a Game

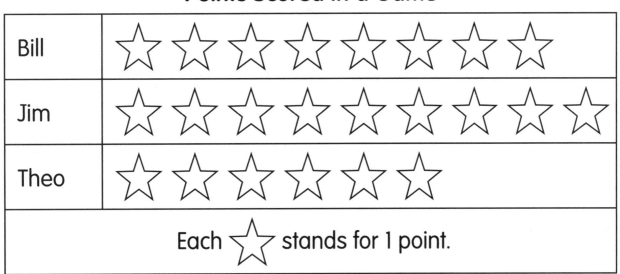

1.   Bill scored _____ points.

2.   _____ scored the most points.

3.   Bill scored _____ more points than Theo.

4.   Theo scored _____ fewer points than Jim.

5.   Bill scored _____ fewer point than Jim.

The picture shows Ben's toys.

Count the toys and draw ◯ to complete the graph.

6.   **Ben's Toys**

Car	Train	Teddy bear	Robot
Each ◯ stands for 1 toy.			

Fill in the blanks.

7. Ben has the greatest number of _____.

8. There are _____ kinds of toys in all.

Name: _____   **Date:** _____

9. He has _____ fewer robots than cars.

10. He has _____ toys in all.

Look at the picture graph.
Then fill in the blanks.

The graph shows the favorite weather of some children.

Favorite Weather

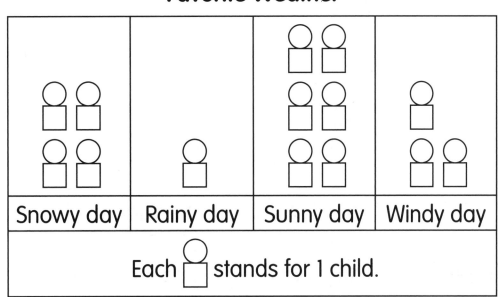

11. _____ children like snowy days.

12. The least number of children like _____ days.

13. _____ more child likes snowy days than windy days.

14. _____ fewer children like rainy days than snowy days.

Name: ____________________ Date: ____________

Look at the picture graph.
Then answer the questions.

The graph shows the types of school lunches of some children.

Types of School Lunches

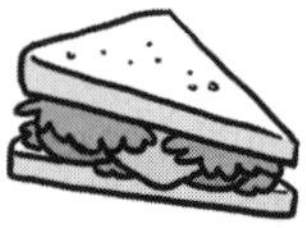 Sandwich	● ● ●
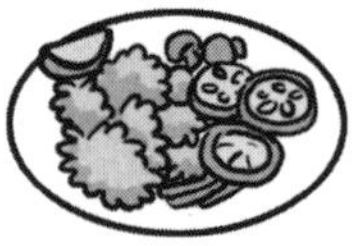 Salad	● ●
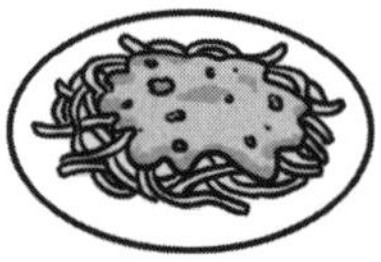 Pasta	● ● ● ● ●
Each ● stands for 1 student.	

15. How many children eat a sandwich for lunch? ________

16. How many children eat pasta or salad for lunch in all?

____

17. How many more children eat pasta than eat a sandwich? ________

18. How many fewer children eat salad than eat pasta? ________

Lesson 3   Tally Charts and Bar Graphs

The picture shows the different things Bella sees in a pond.

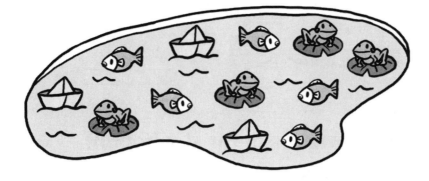

Count the things Bella sees.
Complete the tally chart.
Then fill in the blanks.

1.

Things	Tally	Number
Frog		
Paper boat		
Fish		

2.   There are _____ fish.

3.   There is _____ fewer paper boat than frogs.

4.   There are _____ frogs and fish in all.

Jenna went shopping and bought some pencils, notebooks, pens, and stickers.

The tally chart shows the items she bought.
Complete the tally chart.
Then answer the questions.

5.

Items	Tally	Number
Pencil		
Notebook		
Pen		
Sticker		

6. Which item did she buy the greatest number of?

_____

7. How many stickers did she buy? _____

8. How many more notebooks than pens did she buy?

_____

9. How many pencils did she buy? _____

The picture shows the different animals in a pet shop.

Count the number of animals.
Complete the tally chart.
Then make a bar graph.

10.

Animals	Tally	Number
Kitten		
Puppy		
Parrot		
Goldfish		

11.

Animals in a Pet Shop

Kitten

Puppy

Parrot

Goldfish

Animals

0 1 2 3 4 5 6 7 8
Number of Animals

The tally chart shows how Richard's friends go to school.

Ways	Tally	Number
Bus	ⵑⵑⵑ	5
Bicycle	//	2
Car	////	4

Make a bar graph.
Then answer the questions.

12.

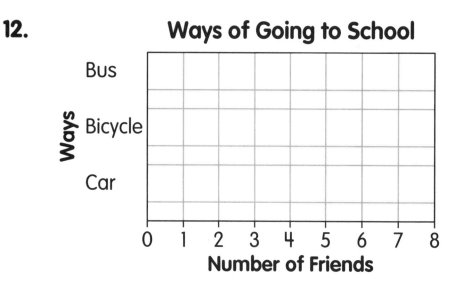

Ways of Going to School

13. How many friends go to school by car? _____

14. How many more friends go to school by bus than

by bicycle? _____

15. How do most of Richard's friends go to school?

_____

Name: _____ **Date:** _____

Put on Your Thinking Cap!

Use the clues and the graph to fill in the blanks.

Crackers can fly. There are 3 such animals.

Puff lives in a hutch. There are 5 such animals.

Bingo has big ears and spots on his body.
There are 6 such animals.

Fluffy has whiskers and a long tail.
There are 4 such animals.

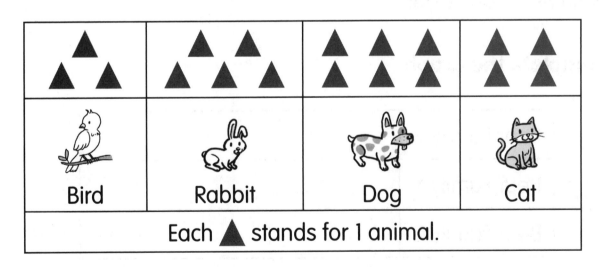

Each ▲ stands for 1 animal.

1. Puff is a _____.

2. Fluffy is a _____.

3. There are _____ more dogs than birds.

The graph shows the number of cubs each Bear Family has.

Bear Family X	Bear Family Y	Bear Family Z

Each stands for 1 cub.

Each cub eats 2 fish.
The graph below shows the total number of fish the cubs in each Bear Family eat.

Complete the graph.

4.

Bear Family X	
Bear Family Y	
Bear Family Z	

Each ◯ stands for 1 fish.

5. How many fish do the cubs eat in all?

They eat _____ fish in all.

CHAPTER 12 Numbers to 40

Lesson 1 Counting to 40

Circle groups of 10.
Then count and write the numbers.

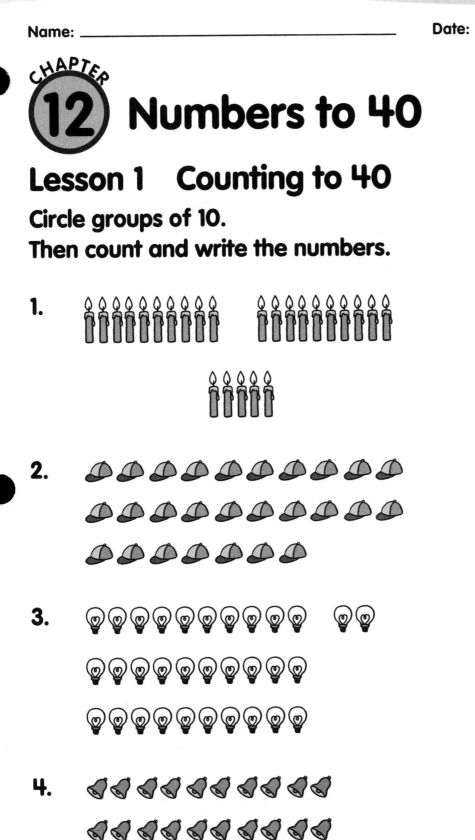

1.

2.

3.

4.

Write the number.

5. twenty-four _____

6. thirty-seven _____

7. forty _____

8. twenty-eight _____

Write the number in words.

9. 22 _____

10. 30 _____

11. 29 _____

12. 38 _____

13. 33 _____

14. 25 _____

Fill in the missing numbers.

15. 30 + 6 = _____

16. _____ + 4 = 24

17. 30 and _____ make 37.

18. 20 and 9 make _____.

19. _____ and 1 make 11.

20. _____ and 5 make 25.

Lesson 2   Place Value

Find the missing numbers.

1.

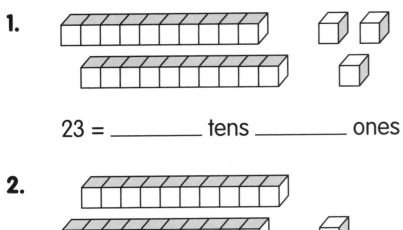

23 = _____ tens _____ ones

2.

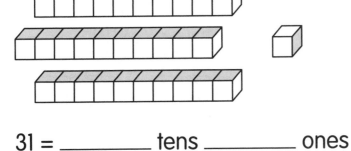

31 = _____ tens _____ ones

Look at the place-value chart.
Write the number it shows.

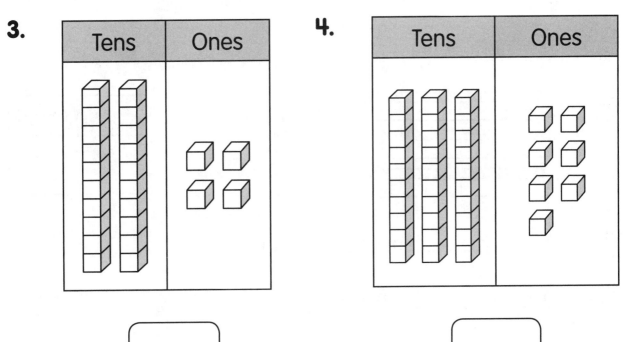

3.

Tens	Ones

4.

Tens	Ones

Count in tens and ones.
Fill in the missing numbers in the place-value charts.
Then fill in the blanks.

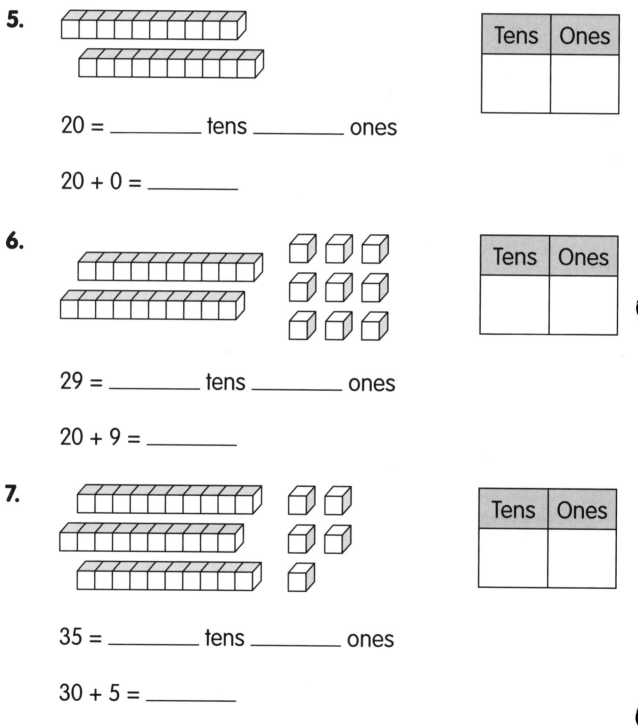

5.

Tens	Ones

20 = _____ tens _____ ones

20 + 0 = _____

6.

Tens	Ones

29 = _____ tens _____ ones

20 + 9 = _____

7.

Tens	Ones

35 = _____ tens _____ ones

30 + 5 = _____

Lesson 3   Comparing, Ordering, and Patterns

Color to show the correct number.
Then fill in the blanks.

1.

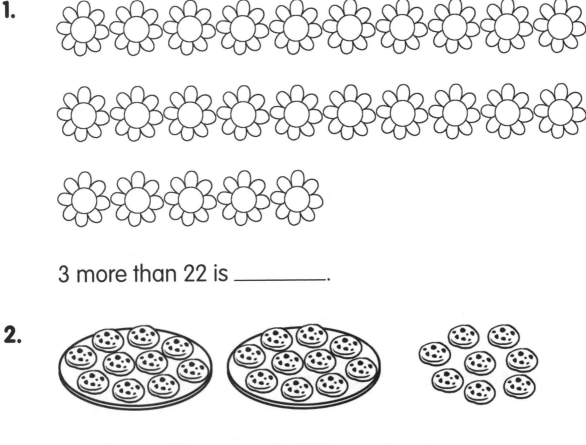

3 more than 22 is _____.

2.

2 less than 28 is _____.

3.

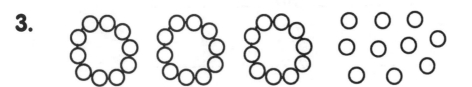

3 less than 40 is _____.

Fill in the blanks.

4. 1 more than 25 is _____.

5. 2 more than 18 is _____.

6. 4 less than 29 is _____.

7. 6 less than 40 is _____.

8. _____ is 5 more than 31.

9. _____ is 8 more than 20.

10. _____ is 2 less than 35.

11. _____ is 10 less than 33.

Complete each number pattern.

12. 34, 35, _____, 37, _____, 39, _____

13. 22, 24, _____, _____, 30, 32, _____

14. 25, 24, _____, _____, 21, 20, _____

15. 40, 38, 36, _____, _____, 30, _____

Name: _____   Date: _____

● **Fill in the blanks using the numbers below.**
Use each number once.

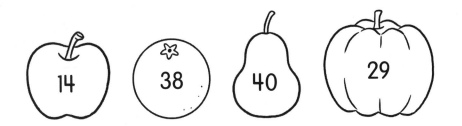

16.   The greatest number is _____.

17.   The least number is _____.

18.   35 is greater than _____.

19.   27 is less than _____.

Fill in the blanks.

20.   Name three numbers that are greater than 27 but less than 35.

_____, _____, _____

21.   Name three numbers that are less than 38 but greater than 26.

_____, _____, _____

22. Match.

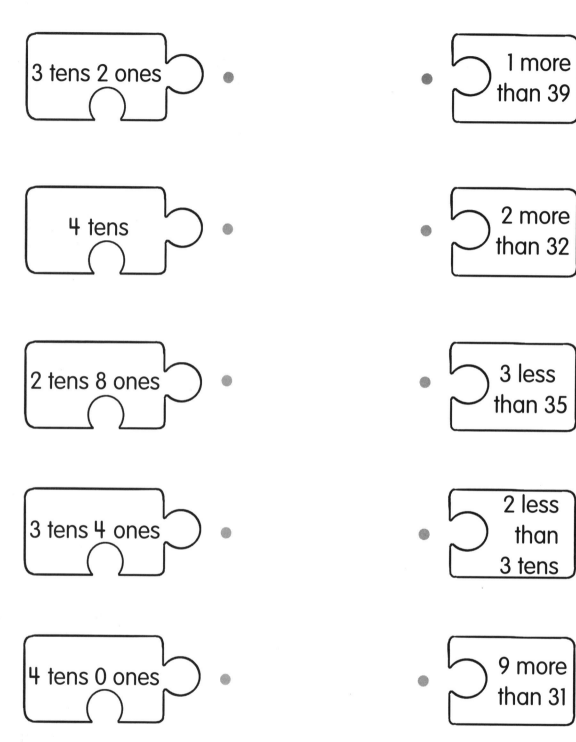

3 tens 2 ones

4 tens

2 tens 8 ones

3 tens 4 ones

4 tens 0 ones

1 more than 39

2 more than 32

3 less than 35

2 less than 3 tens

9 more than 31

● **Fill in the blanks.**

23.

My number is 6 more than the second number.

My number is 4 less than the third number.

My number is 27.

1st Number　　　**2nd Number**　　　**3rd Number**

The first number is _____.

The second number is _____.

24.

My number is 3 more than the third number.

My number is 7 less than the first number.

My number is 36.

1st Number　　　**2nd Number**　　　**3rd Number**

The first number is _____.

The second number is _____.

Complete the number pattern.
Then fill in the blanks.

25.

26. _____ is 5 more than 24.

27. _____ is 6 less than 21.

28. _____ is 8 less than 30.

Put On Your Thinking Cap!

Look at the table.
Complete the table such that every row and column
has the numbers 5, 10, and 15.

Note: Each row and column can contain each number once.
      Use the hints to help you.

1.

Fill in the missing numbers so that the numbers in every row (↔), column (↕), and diagonal (↗) make 30.

2.

16		12
	10	
8		4

 Addition and Subtraction to 40

Lesson 1 Addition Without Regrouping

Circle groups of 10.
Then add by counting on.

1.

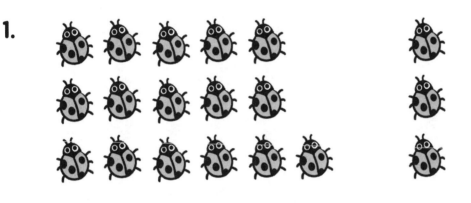

$16 + 3 = $ _____

2.

$33 + 4 = $ _____

Fill in the missing numbers.

3.   21 + 5   = 2 tens _____ one + 5 ones

= 2 tens _____ ones

(20) ( )

= _____

4.   3 + 35   = 3 ones + _____ tens _____ ones

= 3 tens _____ ones

( ) ( )

= _____

5.   26 + 2 = _____ tens _____ ones + 2 ones

= _____ tens 8 ones

( ) ( )

= _____

6.   31 + 4   = _____ tens _____ one + 4 ones

= _____ tens 5 ones

( ) ( )

= _____

Name: _____   Date: _____

Complete each place-value chart.
Then add.

7.

Tens	Ones
3	5
+	4

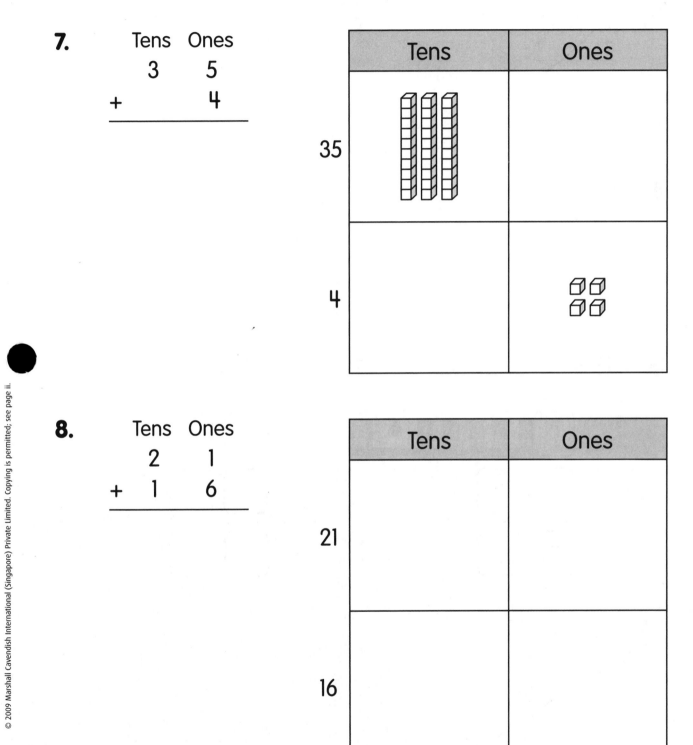

8.

Tens	Ones
2	1
+ 1	6

Add.

9.   2 3
      +   4
      _____

10.   8
      + 2 1
      _____

11.   1 5
      + 2 0
      _____

12.   2 2
      + 1 0
      _____

13. 18 + 21 = _____

14. 25 + 13 = _____

© 2009 Marshall Cavendish International (Singapore) Private Limited. Copying is permitted; see page ii.

Lesson 2   Addition with Regrouping

Fill in the missing numbers.

1.   15 + 9 = 1 ten 5 ones + 9 ones

        = 1 ten 14 ones

        = _____

2.   28 + 8 = _____ tens _____ ones + _____ ones

        = _____ tens _____ ones

        = _____

3.   27 + 6 = _____ tens _____ ones + _____ ones

        = _____ tens _____ ones

        = _____

4.   37 + 3 = _____ tens _____ ones + _____ ones

        = _____ tens _____ ones

        = _____

Add.

5.   2 3
        +   8
        ————————

6.   1 8
        +   9
        ————————

7.   4
        + 3 6
        ————————

8.   5
        + 2 5
        ————————

9.   1 4
        + 1 9
        ————————

10.   2 7
        + 1 7
        ————————

11.   1 6
        + 1 8
        ————————

12.   2 1
        + 1 9
        ————————

Name: _____ **Date:** _____

Fill in the missing numbers.

13. 22 + 9 = _____

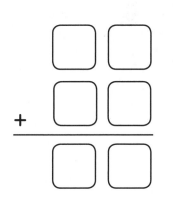

14. 28 + 7 = _____

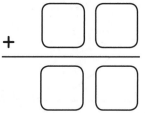

15. 8 + 26 = _____

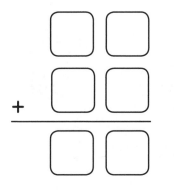

16. 18 + 18 = _____

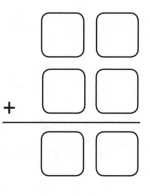

17. 15 + 16 = _____

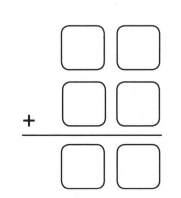

18. 23 + 17 = _____

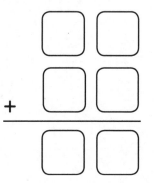

19. **Fill in the blank.**

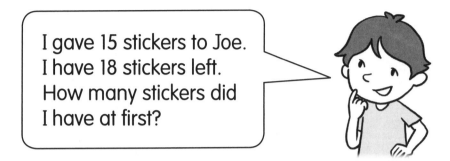

I gave 15 stickers to Joe.
I have 18 stickers left.
How many stickers did
I have at first?

I had _____ stickers at first.

Follow the directions.

20. Circle the answer that is the least.

$$24 + 1 \qquad 8 + 18 \qquad 12 + 19 \qquad 30 + 0$$

21. Circle the answer that is the greatest.

$$9 + 17 \qquad 13 + 18 \qquad 19 + 9 \qquad 29 + 7$$

Lesson 3   Subtraction Without Regrouping

Complete the number bonds.
Then subtract.

1.   27 – 4   = _____

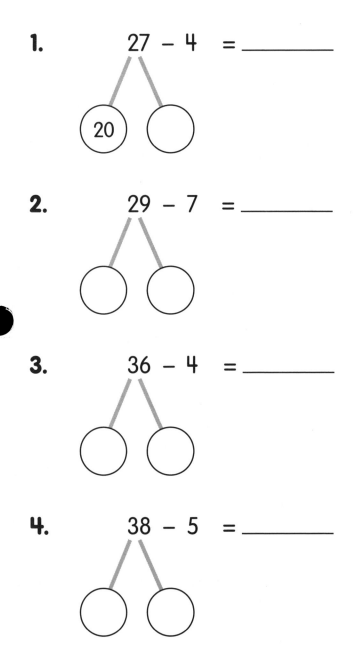

2.   29 – 7   = _____

3.   36 – 4   = _____

4.   38 – 5   = _____

Fill in the missing numbers.

5. 27 – 3 = _____ tens _____ ones – 3 ones

      = 2 tens _____ ones

      = _____

6. 39 – 6 = _____ tens 9 ones – _____ ones

      = _____ tens 3 ones

      = _____

7. 35 – 4 = _____ tens _____ ones – _____ ones

      = _____ tens _____ one

      = _____

Fill in the missing numbers.

8. 2 tens 8 ones – 4 ones = _____ – _____

      = _____

9.   3 tens 7 ones – 2 ones = _____ – _____

= _____

10.   2 tens 6 ones – 1 ten 1 one = _____ – _____

= _____

Subtract.

11.

Tens	Ones
2	8
–	6

12.

Tens	Ones
3	4
–	2

13.

Tens	Ones
3	8
–	8

14.

Tens	Ones
3	7
– 1	5

15.

Tens	Ones
3	3
– 2	1

16.

Tens	Ones
2	9
– 1	0

Fill in the missing numbers.

17.   27 – 5 = _____

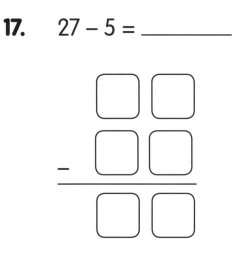

18.   39 – 7 = _____

19.   26 – 15 = _____

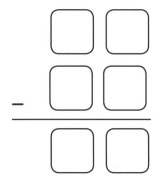

20.   38 – 12 = _____

21.   24 – 14 = _____

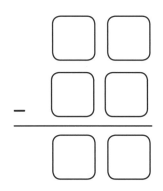

22.   35 – 30 = _____

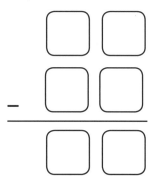

Lesson 4   Subtraction with Regrouping

Subtract.

1.
```
    2 4
  –   6
  _____
```

2.
```
    2 1
  –   9
  _____
```

3.
```
    3 0
  –   8
  _____
```

4.
```
    3 2
  –   5
  _____
```

5.
```
    2 7
  – 1 8
  _____
```

6.
```
    3 3
  – 1 6
  _____
```

7.
```
    3 5
  – 1 9
  _____
```

8.
```
    4 0
  – 1 5
  _____
```

Fill in the missing numbers.

9.   24 − 9 = _____

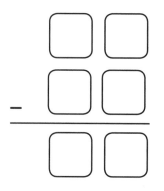

10.   36 − 8 = _____

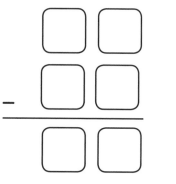

11.   26 − 17 = _____

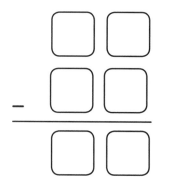

12.   30 − 11 = _____

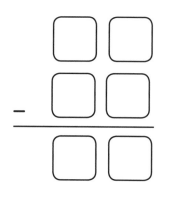

13.   34 − 18 = _____

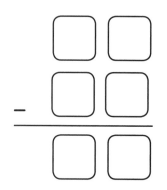

14.   40 − 27 = _____

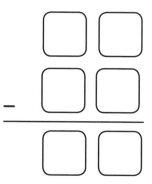

15. Match.

27

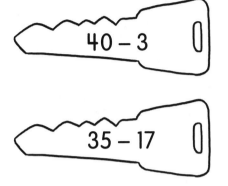
40 – 3

18

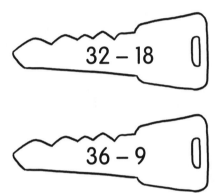
35 – 17

32 – 18

14

36 – 9

37

Subtract.

16. 33 – 7 = _____

17. 34 – 6 = _____

18. 31 – 16 = _____

19. 36 – 19 = _____

Write the missing numbers.

20.

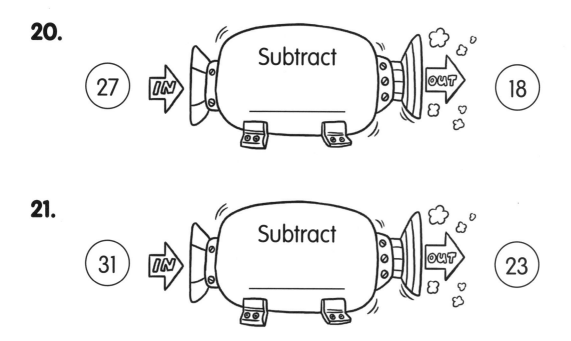

21.

Follow the directions.

22. Circle the answer that is the least.

34 – 18   36 – 17   34 – 8   37 – 8

23. Circle the answer that is the greatest.

14 less than 32   6 less than 33

5 less than 31   15 less than 40

Lesson 5 Adding Three Numbers

Add.

1.

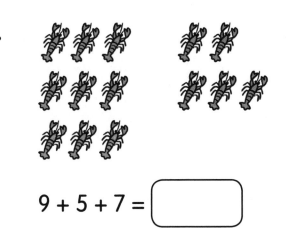

$7 + 3 + 8 =$ ☐

2.

$9 + 5 + 7 =$ ☐

Make ten.
Then add.

3. $7 + 4 + 6 =$ _____

4. $9 + 2 + 5 =$ _____

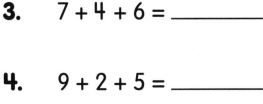

5. $5 + 7 + 9 =$ _____

Add.

6. $8 + 4 + 7 =$ _____ **7.** $6 + 5 + 9 =$ _____

8. **Fill in the missing numbers.**

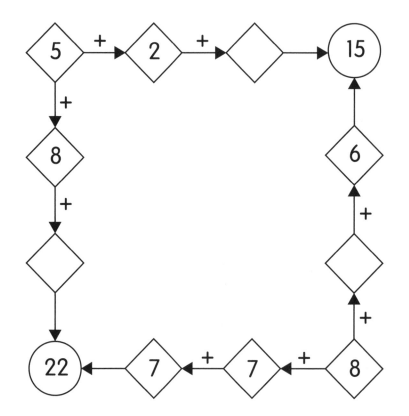

Fill in the blanks with the numbers on the leaves.
Use each number once.

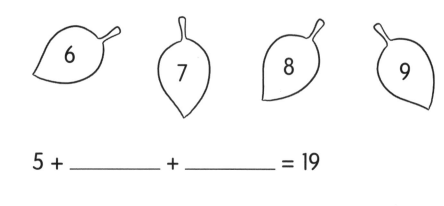

9. $5 +$ _____ $+$ _____ $= 19$

10. $9 +$ _____ $+$ _____ $= 25$

Lesson 6   Real-World Problems: Addition and Subtraction

Solve.

1.   Serene bakes 20 corn muffins.
     She gives away 6 muffins.
     How many muffins does Serene have left?

     Serene has _____ muffins left.

2.   David has 15 stickers in his album.
     He buys 9 more stickers.
     How many stickers does David have in all?

     David has _____ stickers in all.

Solve.

3.   Joanne has 36 marbles in a bag.
      She gives 12 marbles away.
      How many marbles does Joanne have left?

      Joanne has _____ marbles left.

4.   Raul has 27 magnets.
      Eugene has 8 more magnets than Raul.
      How many magnets does Eugene have?

      ⬭ ◯ ⬭ = ⬭

      Eugene has _____ magnets.

Put on Your Thinking Cap!

Fill in the missing numbers.

1. Emily places a ball into the number machine below.
    What happens to the number on the ball?

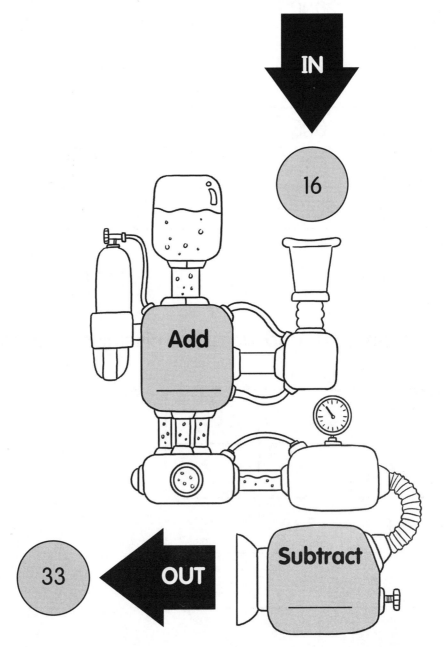

IN

16

Add
_____

Subtract
_____

OUT

33

Fill in the blanks.

2.   In 1999, Joel was 15 years old.
How old will he be in 2012?

Year	Age
1999	15
2000	
2001	
2002	
2003	
⋮	⋮
2012	

He will be _____ years old in 2012.

3.   Find a pattern and write the missing numbers.

38	37	36
36	35	
34	33	

CHAPTER 14 Mental Math Strategies

Lesson 1   Mental Addition

Add mentally.
Use doubles facts.

1.   5 + 6 = _____

2.   4 + 4 = _____

3.   8 + 7 = _____

4.   9 + 9 = _____

5.   6 + 7 = _____

6.   9 + 8 = _____

Add mentally.
First add the ones.
Then add the ones to the tens.

7.   14 + 3 = _____

8.   16 + 2 = _____

9.   11 + 1 = _____

10.   13 + 4 = _____

11.   27 + 2 = _____

12.   21 + 8 = _____

13.   12 + 5 = _____

14.   15 + 3 = _____

15. $26 + 3 =$ _____   **16.** $22 + 4 =$ _____

17. $31 + 3 =$ _____   **18.** $35 + 1 =$ _____

19. $37 + 2 =$ _____   **20.** $34 + 4 =$ _____

Add mentally.
First add the tens.
Then add the tens to the ones.

21. $18 + 10 =$ _____   **22.** $16 + 20 =$ _____

23. $20 + 12 =$ _____   **24.** $10 + 17 =$ _____

25. $25 + 10 =$ _____   **26.** $20 + 14 =$ _____

27. $13 + 10 =$ _____   **28.** $10 + 16 =$ _____

© 2009 Marshall Cavendish International (Singapore) Private Limited. Copying is permitted; see page ii.

Lesson 2   Mental Subtraction

Subtract mentally.
Think of addition.

1. $9 - 4 =$ _____

2. $7 - 3 =$ _____

3. $12 - 5 =$ _____

4. $14 - 6 =$ _____

5. $13 - 9 =$ _____

6. $15 - 7 =$ _____

Subtract mentally.
First subtract the ones.
Then add the ones to the tens.

7. $26 - 3 =$ _____

8. $29 - 7 =$ _____

9. $25 - 4 =$ _____

10. $27 - 3 =$ _____

11. $38 - 5 =$ _____

12. $35 - 4 =$ _____

13. $37 - 6 =$ _____

14. $36 - 2 =$ _____

Subtract mentally.
First subtract the tens.
Then add the tens to the ones.

15.   21 – 10 = _____

16.   28 – 10 = _____

17.   24 – 10 = _____

18.   35 – 10 = _____

19.   32 – 10 = _____

20.   24 – 20 = _____

21.   29 – 20 = _____

22.   37 – 20 = _____

23.   33 – 20 = _____

24.   35 – 30 = _____

25.   39 – 30 = _____

26.   31 – 30 = _____

Put on Your Thinking Cap!

Look at the pattern.
Then fill in the blanks.

1.

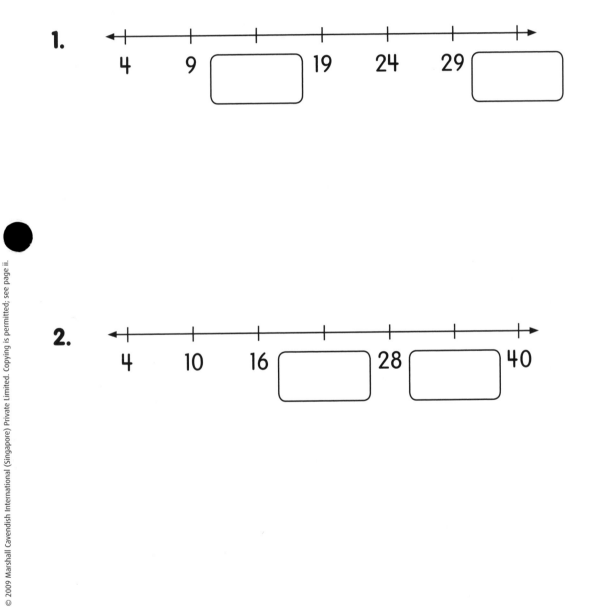

4   9   [   ]   19   24   29   [   ]

2.

4   10   16   [   ]   28   [   ]   40

Fill in the missing numbers.

3.

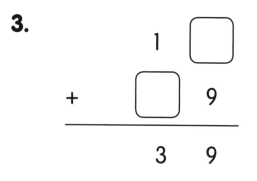

4.

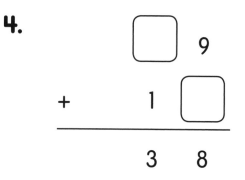

CHAPTER 15 Calendar and Time

Lesson 1   Using a Calendar

Look at the calendar.
Fill in the blanks.

August 2009						
Sunday	Monday	Tuesday	Wednesday	Thursday	Friday	Saturday
						1
2	3	4	5	6	7	8
9	10	11	12	13	14	15
16	17	18	19	20	21	22
23	24	25	26	27	28	29
30	31					

1.   There are _____ days in a week.

2.   August 23, 2009 falls on a _____.

3.   The date of the first Tuesday is _____.

4.   The date of the second Thursday is _____.

5.   The last day of the month is on a _____.

6.   How many days are there in August? _____

7.   The season during the month before August, 2009 is

     _____.

Look at the calendar.
Fill in the blanks.

December 2009						
Sunday	Monday	Tuesday	Wednesday	Thursday	Friday	Saturday
		1	2	3	4	5
6	7	8	9	10	11	12
13	14	15	16	17	18	19
20	21	22	23	24	25	26
27	28	29	30	31		

8. There are _____ days in this month.

9. What day of the week is December 18, 2009?

    _____.

10. The ninth day of the month is on a _____.

11. There are _____ Tuesdays in this month.

12. The date of the first Sunday is _____.

13. The date of the fourth Friday is _____.

14. Which month comes after December? _____

15. The season during the month of December is

    _____.

Lesson 2   Telling Time to the Hour

Fill in the blanks with the correct time.

1.

_____ o'clock

2.

_____ o'clock

3.

_____ o'clock

4.

_____ o'clock

5.

_____ o'clock

6.

_____ o'clock

Fill in the blanks.

This is what Pauline does on Saturday.

7.
Pauline wakes up at

_____.

8.
She eats her breakfast at

_____.

9.
She does her homework at

_____.

10.
She goes to the playground at

_____.

Name: _____ Date: _____

Lesson 3   Telling Time to the Half Hour

Fill in the blanks with the correct time.

Match the clock to the correct time.

1.

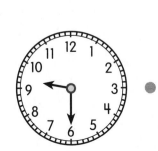

half past 9

half past 4

half past 3

half past 6

2.

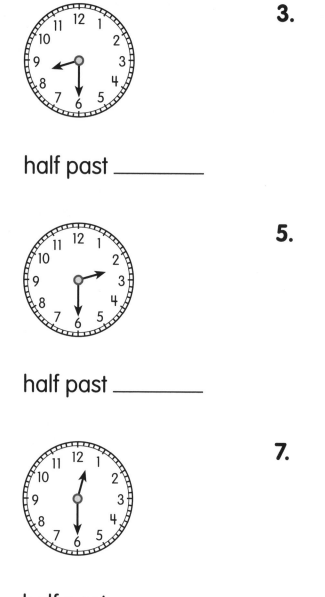

half past _____

3.

half past _____

4.

half past _____

5.

half past _____

6.

half past _____

7.

half past _____

Name: _____   Date: _____

● **Look at the pictures.**
For each correct sentence, put a check (✔) in the box.

8.

The woman bakes a funny clown at 10 o'clock.

9.

The happy clown ran out of the house at half past 11.

10.

The clever clown got a ride from the horse at half past 1.

11. **Look at the pictures.**
Fill in the blanks.
Then write 1, 2, 3, 4, 5, and 6 to show the correct order.

Meg made her sandwiches

at _____.

Meg ate the sandwiches at

the beach at _____.

Meg bought bread and tuna

at a shop at _____.

Meg swam in the sea

at _____.

Meg read her book under a

tree at _____.

Meg went to bed at night

at _____.

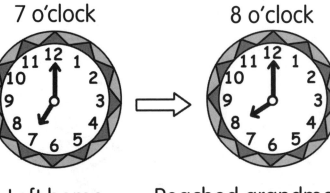 Put on Your Thinking Cap!

Fill in the blanks.

1. Kiri left home at 7 o'clock in the morning.
She took 1 hour to reach her grandmother's house.

7 o'clock   8 o'clock

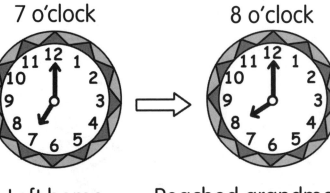

Left home   Reached grandmother's
                          house

Kiri reached her grandmother's house at 8 o'clock.
1 hour after 7 o'clock is 8 o'clock.

Kiri was at her grandmother's house for 3 hours.
At what time did Kiri leave her grandmother's house?

3 hours after 8 o'clock is _____ o'clock.

Kiri left her grandmother's house at _____ o'clock.

2. **Look at the numbers shown on the clock face. Draw a straight line to split the clock face in half. Make sure that the sum of the numbers on each side of the line is equal.**

Hint: The sum of the numbers on each side of the line is between 35 and 40.

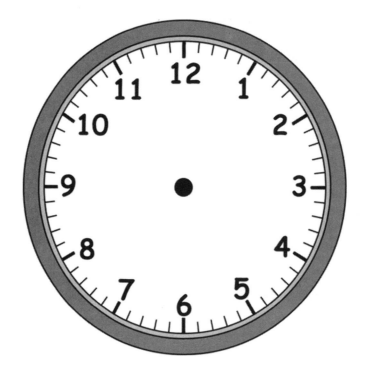

Test Prep

/ 80

for Chapters 10 to 15

Multiple Choice (10 × 2 points = 20 points)

Fill in the circle next to the correct answer.

1. Thirty-four is the same as _____ ones.

   Ⓐ 13   Ⓑ 30   Ⓒ 34   Ⓓ 43

2. Which of the following is the same as 2 tens 6 ones?

   Ⓐ sixteen   Ⓑ twenty

   Ⓒ twenty-six   Ⓓ thirty-six

3. Complete the number pattern.

   The missing number is _____.

   | 30 | 28 | | 24 |

   Ⓐ 32   Ⓑ 26   Ⓒ 22   Ⓓ 20

4. 37 is 10 more than _____.

   Ⓐ 23   Ⓑ 27   Ⓒ 38   Ⓓ 17

5. Charlene goes to the

playground at _____.

Ⓐ 6 o'clock   Ⓑ half past 6

Ⓒ 7 o'clock   Ⓓ half past 7

The graph shows the number of cups of yogurt that John, Peter, Sam, and Carl eat.
Use it to answer Exercises 6 and 7.

Cups of Yogurt Eaten

John	🥛 🥛 🥛 🥛 🥛
Peter	🥛 🥛 🥛 🥛 🥛 🥛
Sam	🥛 🥛 🥛 🥛 🥛 🥛 🥛
Carl	🥛 🥛

Each 🥛 stands for 1 cup of yogurt.

6. _____ eats the most cups of yogurt.

Ⓐ John   Ⓑ Peter   Ⓒ Sam   Ⓓ Carl

7. The boys eat _____ cups of yogurt in all.

Ⓐ 10   Ⓑ 16   Ⓒ 18   Ⓓ 20

Look at the pictures.
Use them to answer Exercises 8 to 10.

Each ▫ stands for 1 unit.

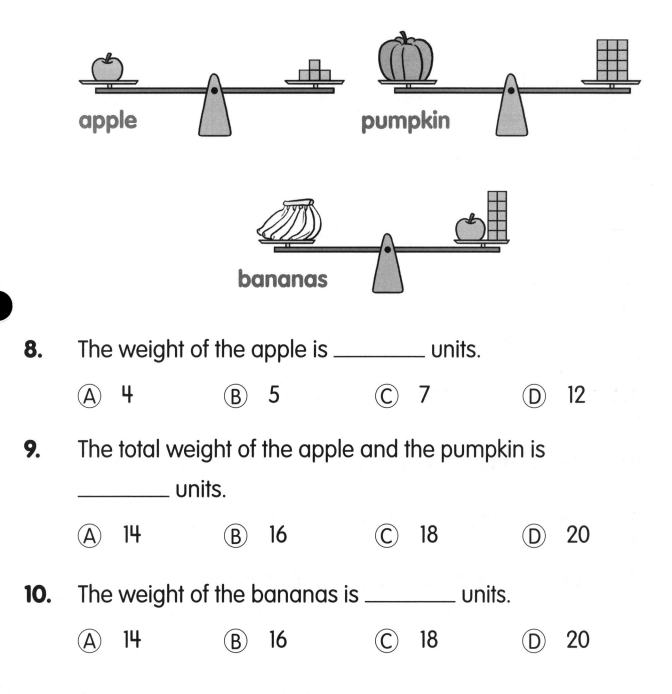

8. The weight of the apple is _____ units.

Ⓐ 4   Ⓑ 5   Ⓒ 7   Ⓓ 12

9. The total weight of the apple and the pumpkin is

_____ units.

Ⓐ 14   Ⓑ 16   Ⓒ 18   Ⓓ 20

10. The weight of the bananas is _____ units.

Ⓐ 14   Ⓑ 16   Ⓒ 18   Ⓓ 20

Short Answer

Fill in the blanks. (2 × 2 points = 4 points)

Each ○ stands for 1 unit.

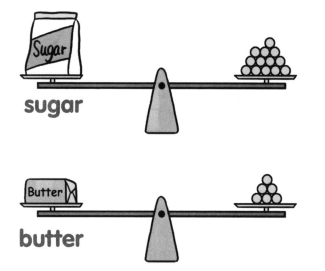

sugar

butter

11. The weight of the bag of sugar is _____ units.

12. The weight of the stick of butter is _____ units.

Fill in the blanks. (2 × 2 points = 4 points)

13. Write 2 tens 7 ones as a number. _____

14. Write the number in Exercise 13 in words. _____

● **The graph shows the number of apples that Lionel, Sean, and Nicole eat from Monday to Wednesday. Use it to answer Exercises 15 to 19.** (5 × 2 points = 10 points)

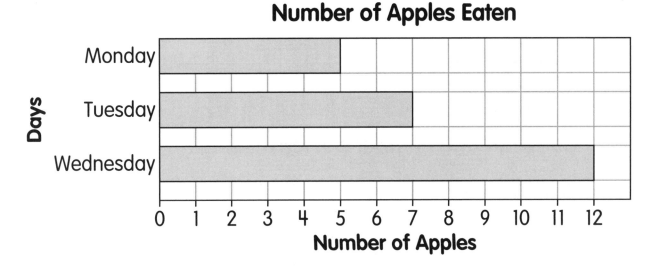

15. They eat the most number of apples on _____.

16. They eat the fewest number of apples on _____.

17. They eat _____ more apples on Wednesday than on Tuesday.

18. They eat _____ fewer apples on Monday than on Wednesday.

19. The three children ate _____ apples in all.

20. **Order the numbers from least to greatest.** (4 points)

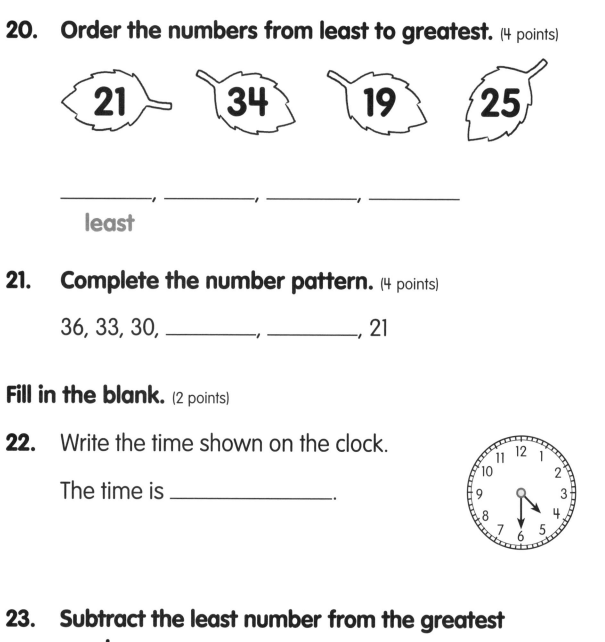

_____, _____, _____, _____
least

21. **Complete the number pattern.** (4 points)

36, 33, 30, _____, _____, 21

Fill in the blank. (2 points)

22. Write the time shown on the clock.

The time is _____.

23. **Subtract the least number from the greatest number.** (6 points)

_____ − _____ = _____

24. **Look at the pictures.**
   Then fill in the blanks. (6 points)

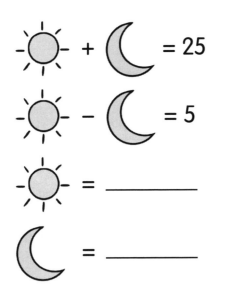

Fill in the blanks. (4 × 2 points = 8 points)

25. _____ months have 30 days.

26. The season during the month of April is _____.

27. Halloween is during the month of _____, during
   the _____ season.

28. If the last day of January is on a Sunday, then the
   first day of February is on a _____.

Extended Response (2 × 6 points = 12 points)
Solve.
Show your work.
Write the number sentence.

29. Mrs. Carlos bakes 24 muffins.
The children eat 9 muffins.
How many muffins are left?

_____ muffins are left.

30. Jessica counts 18 flowers in her front garden.
Then she counts 22 flowers in her back garden.
How many flowers does Jessica count in all?

Jessica counts _____ flowers in all.

CHAPTER 16 Numbers to 100

Lesson 1   Counting

Fill in the blanks.

1.

_____ tens = 30 = thirty

2.

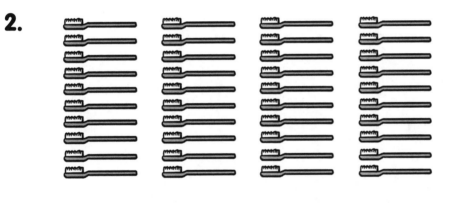

_____ tens = _____ = _____

Count in tens and ones.
Fill in the blanks.

3.

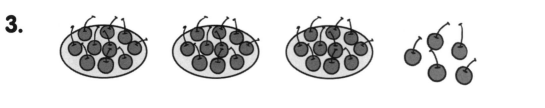

10, … _____, … _____, 31, 32, _____, _____, 35

4.

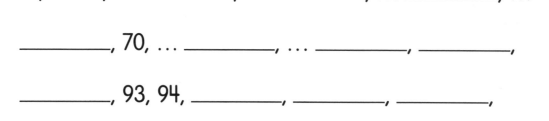

10, … 20, … _____, … _____, … _____, …

_____, 70, … _____, … _____, _____,

_____, 93, 94, _____, _____, _____,

_____

Name: _____ **Date:** _____

● Match the number to the words.

5.

twenty-eight ●

ninety-six ●

eighty-five ●

fifty-seven ●

seventy-two ●

thirty-three ●

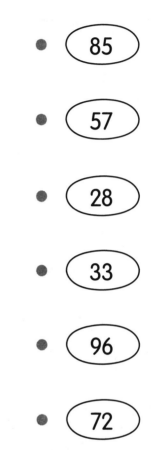

● 85

● 57

● 28

● 33

● 96

● 72

Write the number in words.

6. 76 _____

7. 43 _____

8. 85 _____

9. 67 _____

10. 99 _____

Find the missing numbers.

11. 6 and 80 make _____.

12. 70 and 8 make _____.

13. _____ and 5 make 45.

14. 20 and _____ make 29.

15. 6 + 50 = _____

16. 30 + 7 = _____

Lesson 2   Place Value

Find the missing numbers.

1.

65 = _____ tens _____ ones

65 = 60 + _____

2.

74 = _____ tens _____ ones

74 = _____ + _____

3.

_____ = _____ tens _____ ones

_____ = _____ + _____

Name: ______________________ Date: ______________

Fill in the place-value charts by drawing the correct number of blocks.

4.

Tens	Ones

69

5.

Tens	Ones

81

Count the base-ten blocks.
Fill in the place-value charts.
Then fill in the blanks.

6.

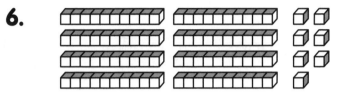

87 = _____ tens _____ ones

80 + 7 = _____

Tens	Ones

7.

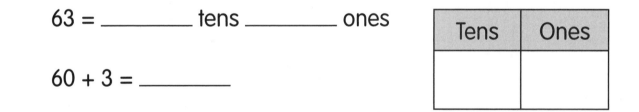

63 = _____ tens _____ ones

60 + 3 = _____

Tens	Ones

8.

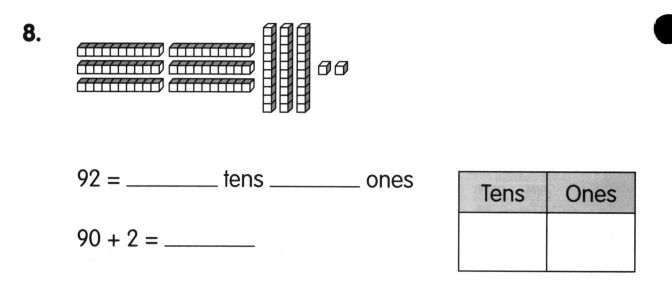

92 = _____ tens _____ ones

90 + 2 = _____

Tens	Ones

Lesson 3   Comparing, Ordering, and Patterns

Look at the pictures.
Then fill in the blanks.

1.

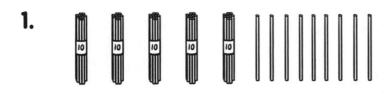

9 more than 50 is _____.

2.

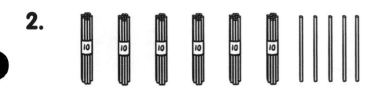

5 less than 70 is _____.

3.

7 less than 90 is _____.

Fill in the blanks.

4.   5 more than 60 is _____.

5.   3 more than 73 is _____.

6.   _____ is 2 more than 80.

7.   _____ is 4 more than 92.

8.   2 less than 58 is _____.

9.   3 less than 64 is _____.

10.   _____ is 5 less than 81.

11.   _____ is 2 less than 100.

Use the numbers to fill in the blanks.

93   78   100   85   62   49

12. The greatest number is _____.

13. The least number is _____.

14. _____ and _____ are less than 78.

15. _____ and _____ are greater than 85.

16. _____ is greater than 49 but less than 78.

Order the numbers from greatest to least.

17.

70   47   32   82

_____, _____, _____, _____

greatest

Complete each number pattern.

18. 30, _____, _____, 60, 70

19. 42, 44, _____, 48, _____, _____

20. 74, 72, _____, _____, 66, _____

21. 80, _____, 70, _____, _____, 55

Put on Your Thinking Cap!

Answer the questions.

1. Sam, Brian, and Shawn find some starfish at the beach.
   How many starfish does each boy find?

I find the same number of starfish as the number of legs on a spider.

Sam

I find 6 more starfish than Sam.

Brian

If Brian gives me 2 of his starfish, I will have 10 starfish in all.

Shawn

How many starfish do the boys find in all?

The boys find _____ starfish in all.

Read each clue.
Find the mystery number.

2.   The mystery number is greater than 40 but less than 50.
     The tens and ones digits are the same.
     What is the mystery number?

     The mystery number is _____.

3.   The mystery number is between 61 and 74.
     The ones digit is 2 more than the tens digit.
     There are 6 tens in the number.
     What is the mystery number?

     The mystery number is _____.

CHAPTER 17 Addition and Subtraction to 100

Lesson 1   Addition Without Regrouping

Add by counting on.

1.   65 + 4 = _____

65, 66, _____, _____, _____

2.   53 + 5 = _____

53, _____, _____, _____, _____, _____

Add.

3. $\begin{array}{r} 7\ 3 \\ +\ \ \ 6 \\ \hline \end{array}$

4. $\begin{array}{r} 5 \\ +\ 6\ 2 \\ \hline \end{array}$

5. $\begin{array}{r} 4\ 0 \\ +\ 2\ 5 \\ \hline \end{array}$

6. $\begin{array}{r} 3\ 5 \\ +\ 5\ 3 \\ \hline \end{array}$

Fill in the missing numbers.

7. 8 + 61 = _____

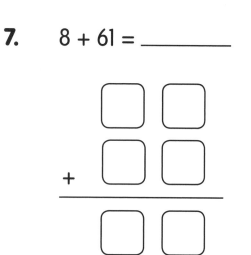

8. 74 + 4 = _____

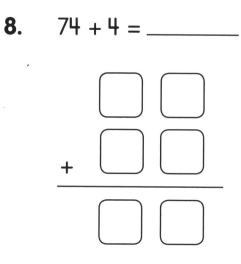

9. 20 + 66 = _____

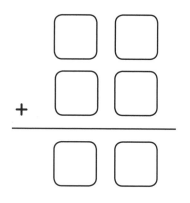

10. 27 + 50 = _____

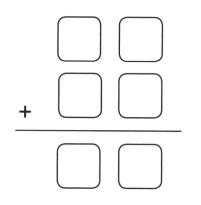

11. 58 + 21 = _____

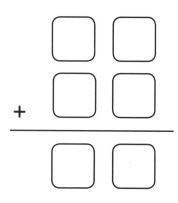

12. 16 + 82 = _____

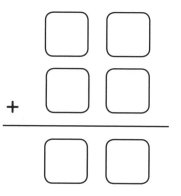

Lesson 2   Addition with Regrouping
Add.

1.
```
    4 3
  +   8
  _____
```

2.
```
    5 6
  +   9
  _____
```

3.
```
      5
  + 6 7
  _____
```

4.
```
      7
  + 4 8
  _____
```

5.
```
    5 7
  + 3 3
  _____
```

6.
```
    6 9
  + 2 4
  _____
```

7.
```
    4 3
  + 4 8
  _____
```

8.
```
    8 5
  + 1 5
  _____
```

Fill in the missing numbers.

9.   64 + 16 = _____

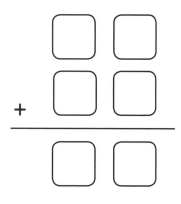

10.   27 + 34 = _____

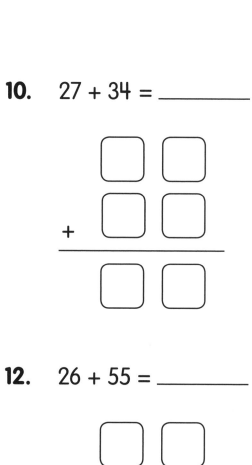

11.   48 + 35 = _____

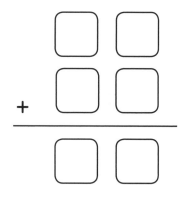

12.   26 + 55 = _____

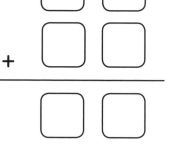

13.   51 + 29 = _____

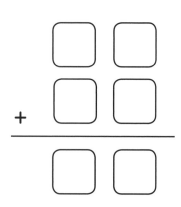

14.   77 + 17 = _____

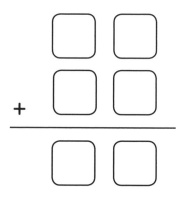

Name: _____   Date: _____

Match.

15.

| 48 + 35 | ● | | ● | 71 |

| 88 + 12 | ● | | ● | 93 |

| 67 + 26 | ● | | ● | 83 |

| 13 + 58 | ● | | ● | 100 |

| 37 + 15 | ● | | ● | 81 |

| 42 + 28 | ● | | ● | 52 |

| 64 + 17 | ● | | ● | 70 |

Name: _____   Date: _____

Add.
Then answer the question.

16. 18 + 64 = _____ (N)

17. 6 + 35 = _____ (T)

18. 27 + 36 = _____ (O)

19. 49 + 23 = _____ (I)

20. 5 + 78 = _____ (D)

21. 9 + 82 = _____ (A)

22. 52 + 48 = _____ (T)

23. 7 + 87 = _____ (C)

What is the message?

Match the letters to the answers below to find out.

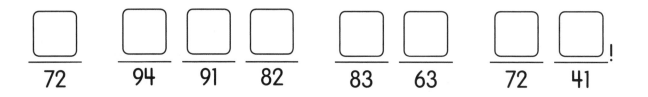

72   94   91   82   83   63   72   41 !

Name: _____ **Date:** _____

Lesson 3   Subtraction Without Regrouping

Subtract.

1.
```
    5  7
 -     4
 _____
```

2.
```
    8  8
 -     6
 _____
```

3.
```
    9  9
 -  7  0
 _____
```

4.
```
    6  5
 -  3  3
 _____
```

5. 45 – 3 = _____

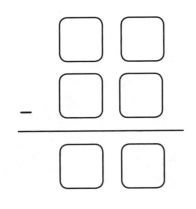

6. 79 – 8 = _____

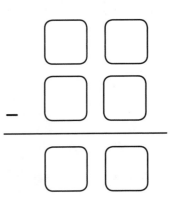

7. 68 – 50 = _____

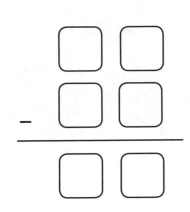

8. 86 – 22 = _____

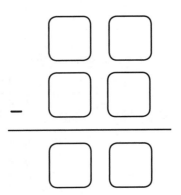

Name: _____

Date: _____

Match.

9.

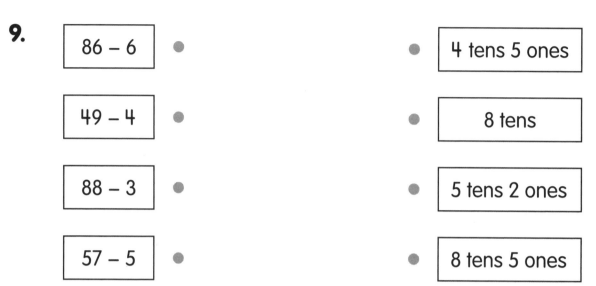

| 86 – 6 | ● | ● | 4 tens 5 ones |

| 49 – 4 | ● | ● | 8 tens |

| 88 – 3 | ● | ● | 5 tens 2 ones |

| 57 – 5 | ● | ● | 8 tens 5 ones |

Follow the directions.

10. Circle the least answer.

48 – 22   76 – 43   56 – 23   87 – 44

11. Circle the greatest answer.

69 – 17   67 – 5   88 – 42   94 – 23

Lesson 4   Subtraction with Regrouping
Subtract.

1.
```
    7 1
  -   6
  _____
```

2.
```
    6 2
  -   8
  _____
```

3.
```
    5 0
  - 1 3
  _____
```

4.
```
    8 5
  - 2 7
  _____
```

5.   24 – 7 = _____

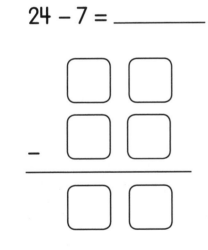

6.   56 – 9 = _____

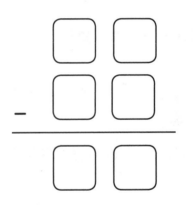

7.   80 – 45 = _____

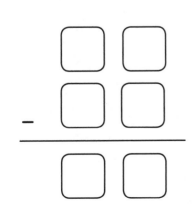

8.   71 – 28 = _____

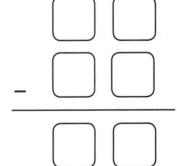
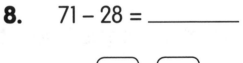

Match.

9.

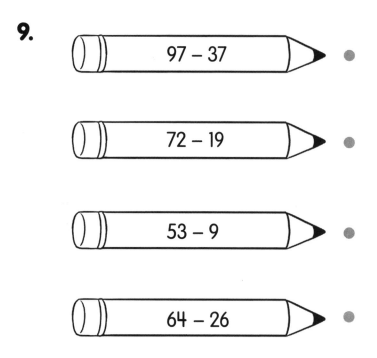

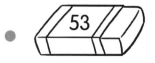

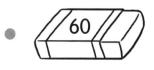

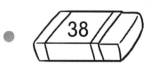

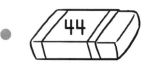

Find the numbers.

10. Subtract 2 from 30.

11. Take away 27 from 84.

12. Subtract 3 tens 5 ones from 8 tens.

13. What number is 18 less than 65?

14. What number is 25 less than 43?

Name: _____   Date: _____

  Match.

15.

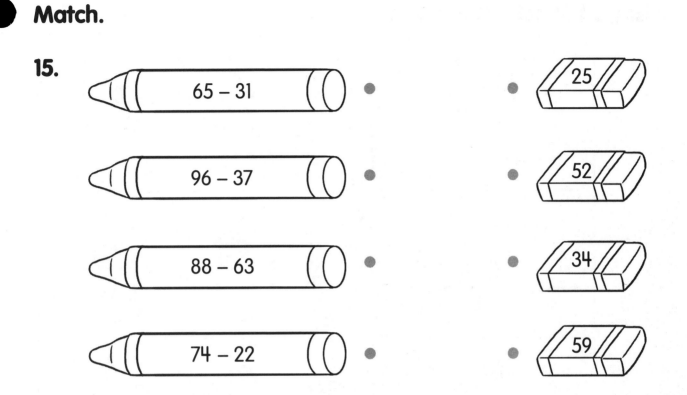

65 – 31   •   • 25

96 – 37   •   • 52

88 – 63   •   • 34

74 – 22   •   • 59

Color the correct answer.

16.

99 – 17	83	82	73
73 – 58	15	26	17
82 – 47	35	27	25

Name: _____   Date: _____

Circle the correct answer.

17.

63 − 19	92	44	56
74 − 28	48	37	46
56 − 37	19	17	29
83 − 44	27	39	36
90 − 73	16	21	17

☀️ Put on Your Thinking Cap!

Fill in the blanks.

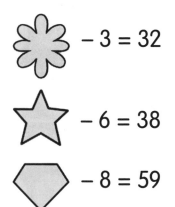 $- 3 = 32$

☆ $- 6 = 38$

⬠ $- 8 = 59$

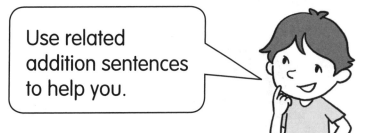

> Use related addition sentences to help you.

1. $=$ _____

2. ☆ $=$ _____

3. ⬠ $=$ _____

4. ☆ $-$ ✽ $=$ _____

5. ⬠ $-$ ✽ $=$ _____

6. ⬠ $-$ ☆ $=$ _____

Find the numbers.

7.   I add 20 to my number and subtract 17 from the
new number.
The answer is 37.
What is my number?

My number is _____.

8.   I add 32 to my number and subtract 26 from the
new number.
The answer is 74.
What is my number?

My number is _____.

CHAPTER 18 Multiplication and Division

Lesson 1 Adding the Same Number

Look at the pictures.
Then fill in the blanks.

1.

_____ + _____ + _____ + _____ = _____

_____ twos = _____

There are _____ frogs in all.

Draw.
Then fill in the blanks.

2. There are 5 bowls.
    Draw 4 marbles in each bowl.

5 fours = _____

There are _____ marbles in all.

3. There are 4 bowls.
Draw 6 marbles in each bowl.

4 _____ = _____

There are _____ marbles in all.

Match.

4.

8 + 8 + 8 + 8 + 8

6 + 6 + 6 + 6

9 + 9 + 9

3 nines

5 eights

4 sixes

40

27

24

● Lesson 2   Sharing Equally

Look at the picture.
Then fill in the blanks.

1.

There are _____ crackers in all.

There are _____ plates.

There are _____ crackers on each plate.

● Circle the correct number of objects.
Then fill in the blanks.

2.   Put 8 eggs into 2 equal groups.

There are _____ eggs in each group.

3.   Put 15 strawberries into 3 equal groups.

There are _____ strawberries in each group.

© 2009 Marshall Cavendish International (Singapore) Private Limited. Copying is permitted; see page ii.

Circle.
Then fill in the blanks.

4. Mrs. Crocker gives 10 apples to 2 boys.
Each boy gets the same number of apples.
How many apples does each boy get?

Each boy gets _____ apples.

5. 3 girls catch 12 butterflies.
Each girl catches the same number of butterflies.
How many butterflies does each girl catch?

Each girl catches _____ butterflies.

⬤ **Circle.**
Then fill in the blanks.

6. Share 18 tarts equally among 6 children.
How many tarts does each child get?

Each child gets _____ tarts.

7. Mrs. Tilley has 20 flowers.
She shares the flowers equally among her 4 daughters.
How many flowers does each daughter get?

Each daughter gets _____ flowers.

Name: _____ **Date:** _____

Look at the picture.
Then fill in the blanks.

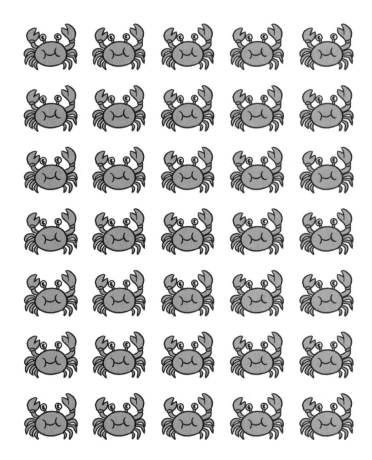

8. How many crabs are there in all?

    There are _____ crabs in all.

9. Mr. Peters puts all the crabs in 7 tanks.
    He puts the same number of crabs in each tank.
    How many crabs are there in each tank?

    There are _____ crabs in each tank.

● Lesson 3   Finding the Number of Groups

Fill in the blanks.

1.

Calvin buys 16 pears.

He puts _____ pears in each bag.

He needs _____ bags.

2.

Kim buys 24 oranges.

She puts _____ oranges in each bag.

She needs _____ bags.

Circle.
Then fill in the blanks.

3.   There are 15 stamps.
Circle groups of 3.

There are _____ groups of 3 stamps.

4.   There are 14 gloves.
Circle groups of 2.

There are _____ groups of 2 gloves.

● Circle.
Then fill in the blanks.

5. Mary has 15 bracelets.
She gives 3 bracelets to each friend.
How many friends are there?

There are _____ friends.

6. Joel has 20 stickers.
He pastes 2 stickers on each page.
How many pages does he need?

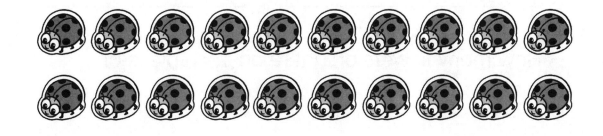

He needs _____ pages.

7.   There are 8 flowers and 2 pieces of paper.
Draw an equal number of flowers on each piece
of paper.

How many flowers are there on each piece of

paper? _____

Put on Your Thinking Cap!

Read the story.
Answer the questions.

1. Luis has 9 red marbles.
    He also has 6 yellow marbles.
    He puts the marbles into 3 equal groups.
    Each group has the same number of red marbles and
    yellow marbles.
    a. How many red marbles are there in each group?
    b. How many yellow marbles are there in each group?

    Draw marbles to help you find the answer.

Red		
Yellow		

a. There are _____ red marbles in each group.

b. There are _____ yellow marbles in each group.

Read the story.
Fill in the blank.

2.   Lynette has less than 20 stickers.
      If she puts the stickers in groups of 4, she has
      3 stickers left over.
      Find the most stickers Lynette can have.

      Draw stickers to help you find the answer.

      The most stickers Lynette can have is _____.

CHAPTER 19 Money

Lesson 1   Penny, Nickel, and Dime

Match.

1.   1¢ •   •  •   • nickel

     5¢ •   •   •   • penny

     10¢ •   •   •   • dime

Find the value of the group of pennies.
Then circle the name of the coin that has the same value.

2.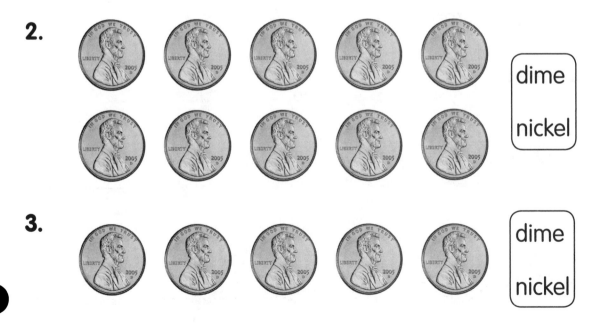

dime

nickel

3.

dime

nickel

Group the pennies, nickels, and dimes.
Then count.

4.

_____ pennies

_____ nickels

_____ dimes

Find the value.

5.

_____ ¢

6.

_____ ¢

Find the value in each purse.

7.

 ¢

8.

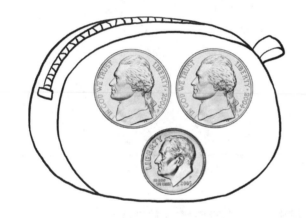

 ¢

9.

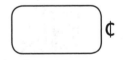 ¢

Circle the correct number of coins to equal the value.

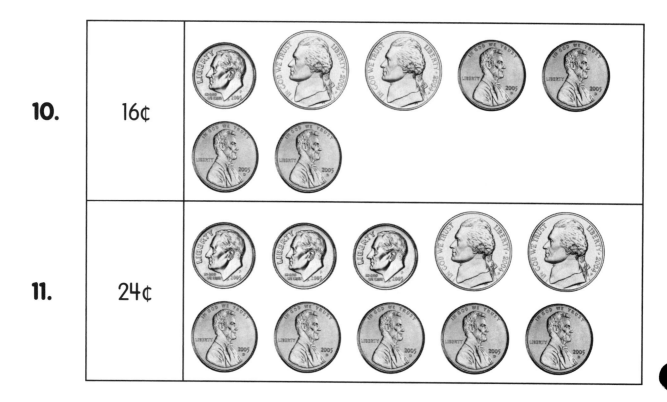

10. 16¢	
11. 24¢	

Is there enough money to buy the items shown?
Circle *yes* or *no*.

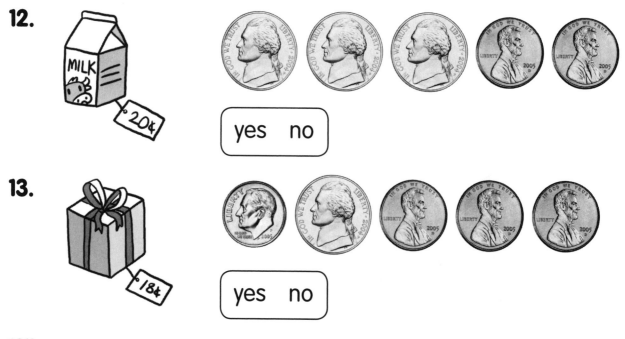

12.

yes   no

13.

yes   no

Lesson 2   Quarter

Fill in the missing number.

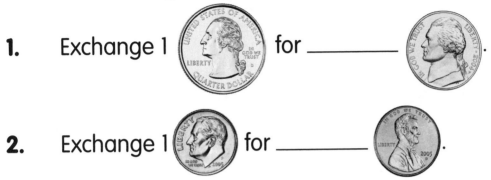

1. Exchange 1 [quarter] for _____ [nickel] .

2. Exchange 1 [dime] for _____ [penny] .

Which group of coins can you exchange for a quarter?
Check (✔) the correct boxes.

3.

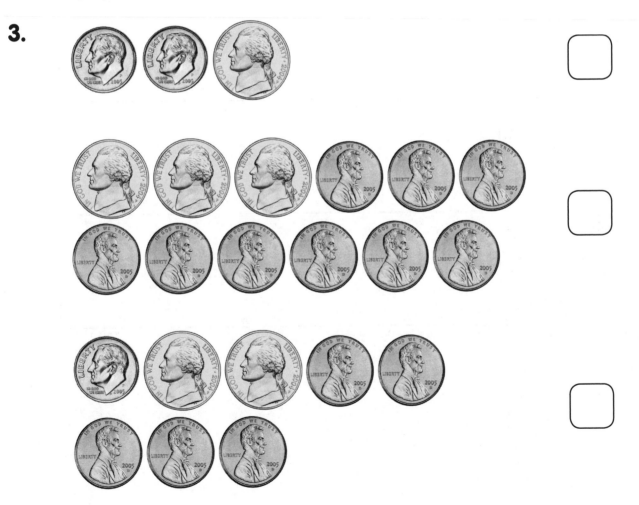

Draw pennies (**1¢**)**, nickels** (**5¢**)**, dimes** (**10¢**) **and quarters** (**25¢**) **to show ways to exchange a quarter.**

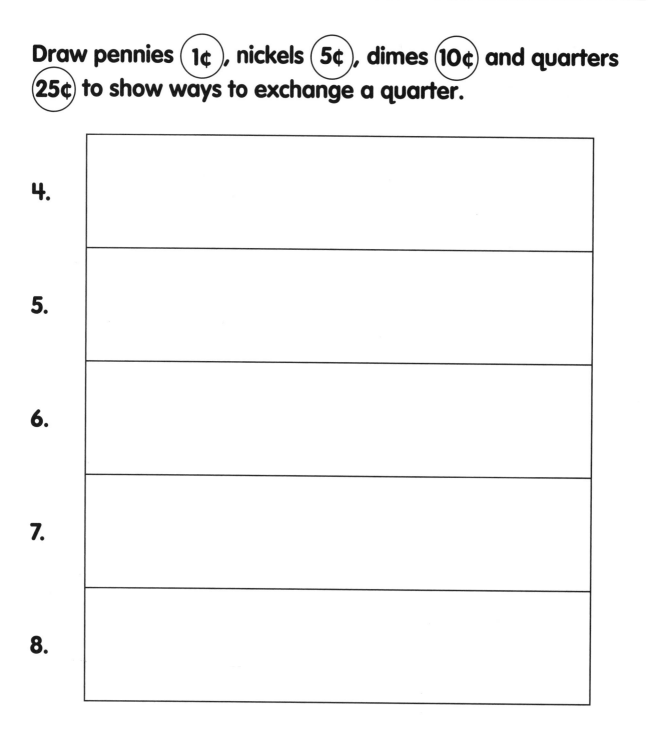

4.

5.

6.

7.

8.

Lesson 3   Counting Money

Write the amount of money in numbers.

1.   seventy cents _____

2.   thirty cents _____

3.   sixty-five cents _____

4.   eighty-nine cents _____

5.   Fifty cents has a value of _____.

Which set has less money?
Check (✓) the box.

6.

Complete the chart to show the number of each coin needed to make $1.

7.

Using 4 coins	4			
Using 6 coins				
Using 7 coins				
Using 10 coins				
Using 12 coins				
Using 100 coins				

Name: _____ **Date:** _____

Circle the coins you need to buy each thing.

8.

33¢

9.

56¢

10.

60¢

Use pennies $1¢$, nickels $5¢$, dimes $10¢$, and quarters $25¢$.

Draw 2 ways to pay for each item.

11.

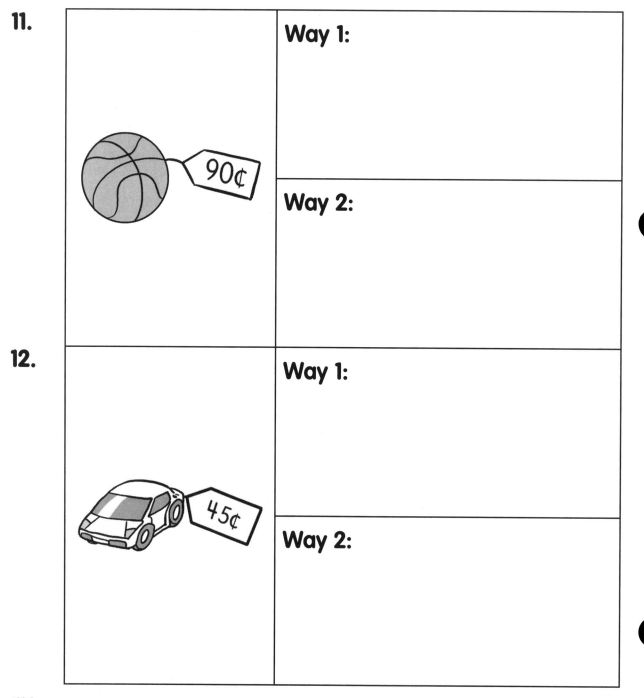

Way 1:

Way 2:

12.

Way 1:

Way 2:

Lesson 4 Adding and Subtracting Money

Add.

1.

15¢ + 50¢ = _____¢

2.

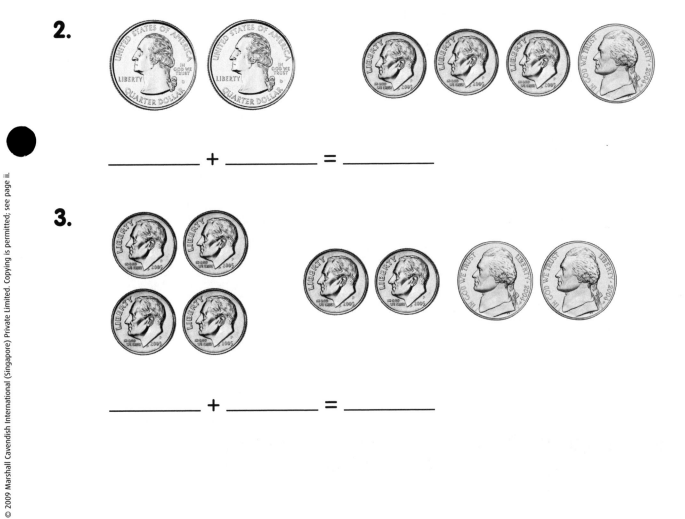

_____ + _____ = _____

3.

_____ + _____ = _____

Three children bought some items during a sale.

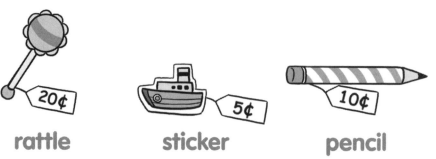

rattle   sticker   pencil

Fill in the correct amount that each child spends.

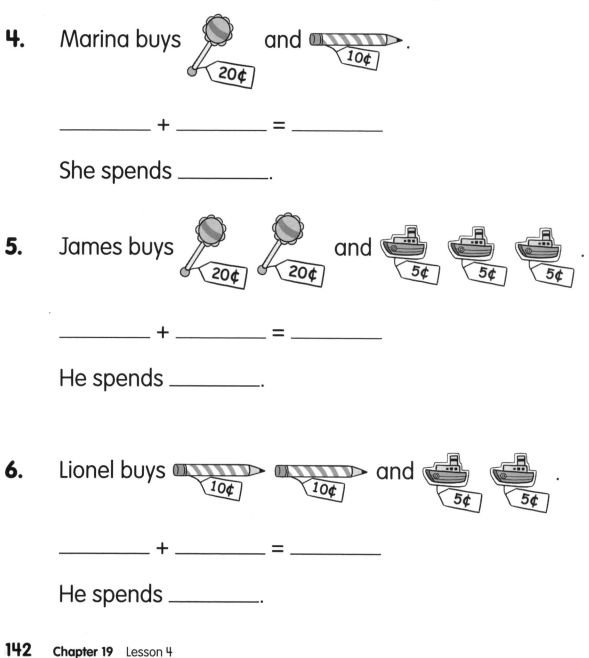

4.   Marina buys [rattle 20¢] and [pencil 10¢].

_____ + _____ = _____

She spends _____.

5.   James buys [rattle 20¢] [rattle 20¢] and [sticker 5¢] [sticker 5¢] [sticker 5¢].

_____ + _____ = _____

He spends _____.

6.   Lionel buys [pencil 10¢] [pencil 10¢] and [sticker 5¢] [sticker 5¢].

_____ + _____ = _____

He spends _____.

7. Circle the greatest number of different items Amy can buy with 90¢.

Subtract.

8. 85¢ – 20¢ = _____

9. 57¢ – 35¢ = _____

10. 70¢ – 48¢ = _____

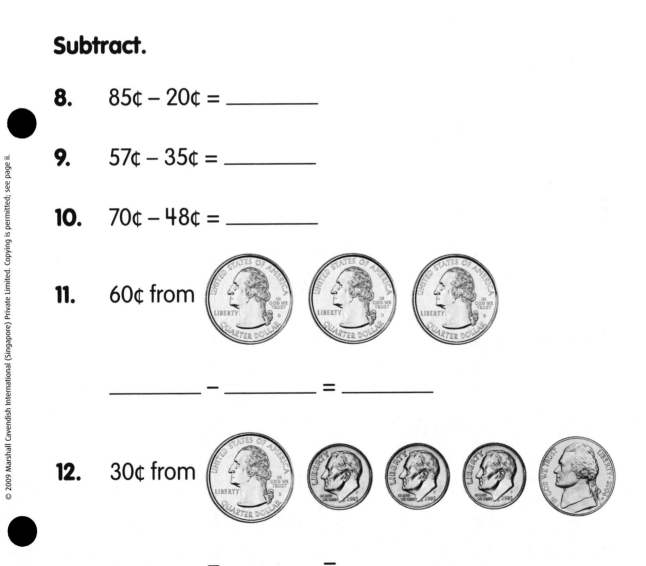

11. 60¢ from

_____ – _____ = _____

12. 30¢ from

_____ – _____ = _____

Complete the table.

	You Have	You Buy	Your Change
13.		ruler 45¢	50¢ – 45¢ =
14.		GLUE 60¢ glue	
15.		basketball 90¢	
16.		book 39¢	

Solve.

17. Ria has 50¢.
She buys a bracelet and a necklace.
How much money does she have left?

She has _____ left.

18. Tom buys the items shown.
How much does he spend in all?

He spends _____ in all.

Name: _____   Date: _____

Solve.

19. Carmen buys a box of crayons.
Gomez buys an eraser.
How much more does Carmen pay
than Gomez?

Carmen pays _____ more than Gomez.

20. David buys a notebook.
He has 13¢ left.
How much did David have at first?

He had _____ at first.

Put on Your Thinking Cap!

Fill in the blanks.

The items below are sold in Uncle Ben's shop.

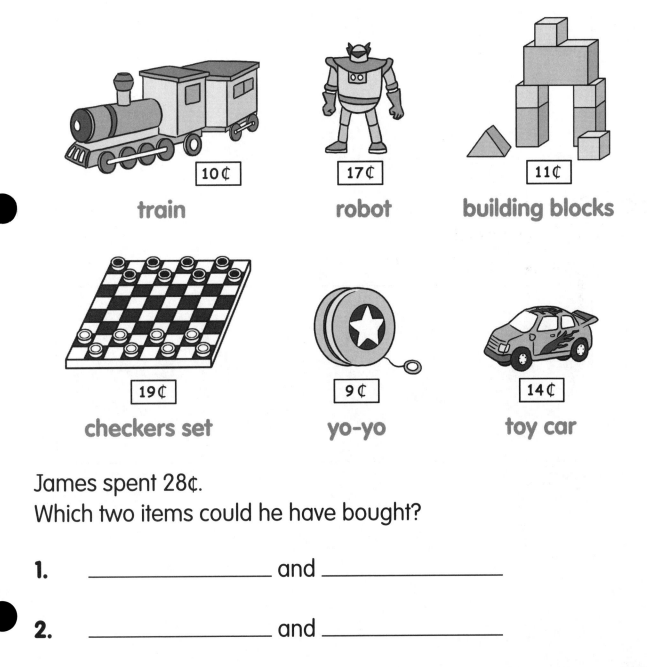

10¢	17¢	11¢
train	**robot**	**building blocks**
19¢	9¢	14¢
checkers set	**yo-yo**	**toy car**

James spent 28¢.
Which two items could he have bought?

1. _____ and _____

2. _____ and _____

Solve.

3.   Sarah, Amy, Neil, and Pedro have 34 coins in all.
Each group of coins belongs to a different child.

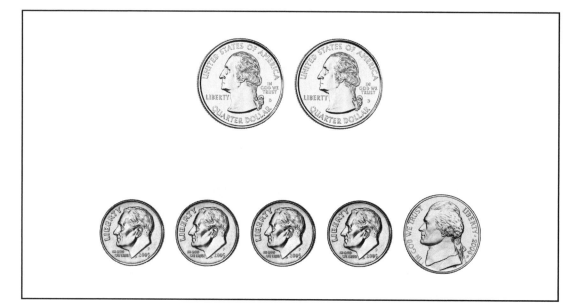

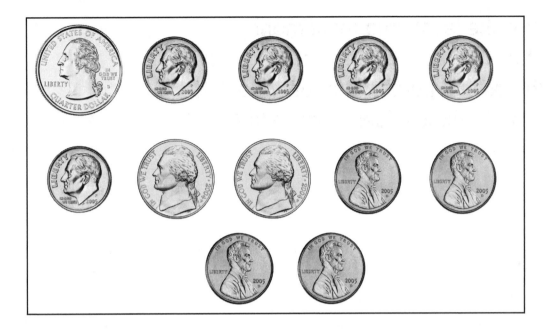

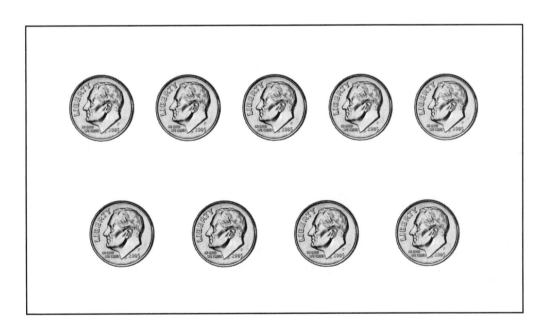

Neil has the least amount of money.
Amy has the greatest amount of money.
Sarah has the greatest number of coins.
How much money does each child have?

Sarah   Amy   Neil   Pedro

_____   _____   _____   _____

End-of-Year Test Prep

Multiple Choice (20 × 2 points = 40 points)

Fill in the circle next to the correct answer.

1. 4 tens 4 ones is the same as _____.

Ⓐ 14   Ⓑ 40   Ⓒ 42   Ⓓ 44

2. 84 is 10 more than _____.

Ⓐ 60   Ⓑ 74   Ⓒ 85   Ⓓ 94

3. 57 − 3 = ☐

Ⓐ 52   Ⓑ 54   Ⓒ 60   Ⓓ 73

4.

> I have 18 balloons.

> I have 5 more balloons than you.

Johnson   Sheena

Sheena has _____ balloons.

Ⓐ 5   Ⓑ 13   Ⓒ 18   Ⓓ 23

5.

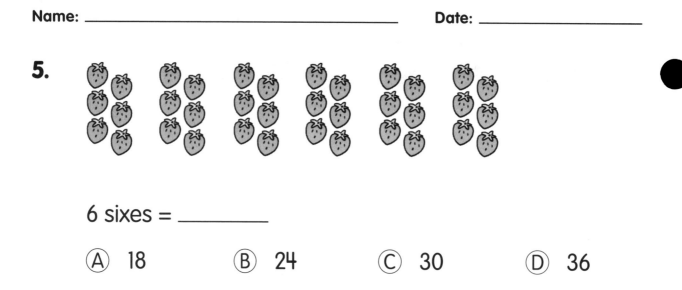

6 sixes = _____

(A) 18　　　(B) 24　　　(C) 30　　　(D) 36

6. Share 12 bananas equally among 4 children.

Each child gets _____ bananas.

(A) 2　　　(B) 3　　　(C) 4　　　(D) 8

7.

5 threes = _____

(A) 25　　　(B) 20　　　(C) 16　　　(D) 15

8.

The ribbon is about _____ ⊂⊃ long.

(A) 12   (B) 11   (C) 10   (D) 8

9.

caterpillar   snail   turtle   frog   crab   ladybug

The _____ is 5th from the right.

(A) crab   (B) snail   (C) frog   (D) turtle

10. The value of the coins is _____ in all.

(A) 58¢   (B) 55¢   (C) 53¢   (D) 50¢

11.

Each ○ stands for 1 unit.

The weight of the ball is _____ units.

(A) 3   (B) 5   (C) 6   (D) 9

12.

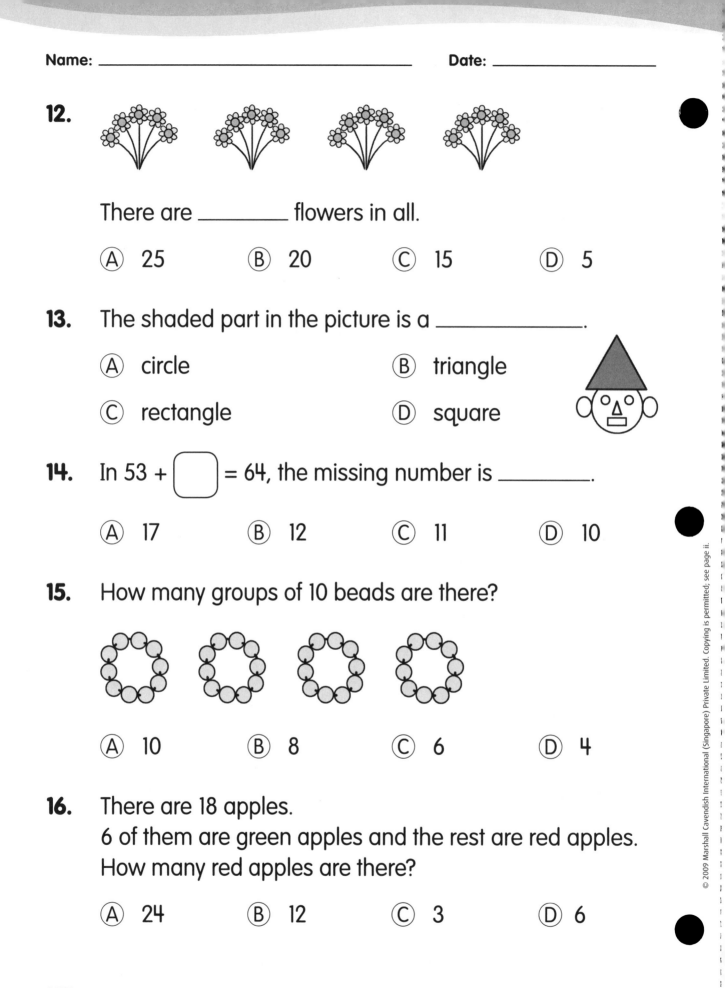

There are _____ flowers in all.

(A) 25   (B) 20   (C) 15   (D) 5

13. The shaded part in the picture is a _____.

(A) circle   (B) triangle

(C) rectangle   (D) square

14. In 53 + ☐ = 64, the missing number is _____.

(A) 17   (B) 12   (C) 11   (D) 10

15. How many groups of 10 beads are there?

(A) 10   (B) 8   (C) 6   (D) 4

16. There are 18 apples.
6 of them are green apples and the rest are red apples.
How many red apples are there?

(A) 24   (B) 12   (C) 3   (D) 6

© 2009 Marshall Cavendish International (Singapore) Private Limited. Copying is permitted; see page ii.

● **The graph shows the flowers in Lynn's garden.**
Use the graph to answer Exercises 17 and 18.

Flowers in Lynn's Garden

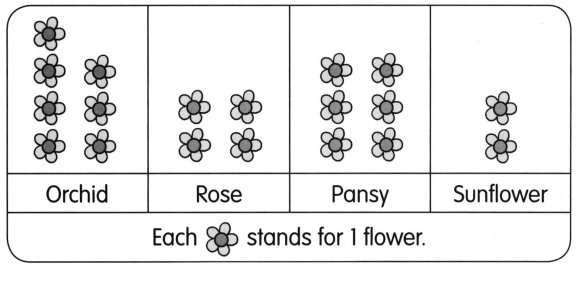

| Orchid | Rose | Pansy | Sunflower |

Each 🌼 stands for 1 flower.

17. Lynn has _____ fewer roses than pansies.

    Ⓐ 1   Ⓑ 2   Ⓒ 3   Ⓓ 4

18. She has the greatest number of _____.

    Ⓐ orchids

    Ⓑ roses

    Ⓒ pansies

    Ⓓ sunflowers

19.   4 + 4 + 4 + 4 + 4 = _____ fours

(A) 1   (B) 2   (C) 4   (D) 5

20.   There are 3 girls.
Mrs. Sommers gives each girl 10 crackers.
How many crackers does Mrs. Sommers give
away in all?

(A) 30   (B) 13   (C) 10   (D) 7

Short Answer

Write the number in words. (2 points)

21.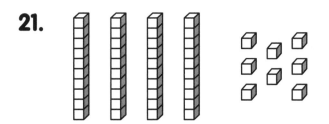

_____

22.   Order the numbers from greatest to least. (2 points)

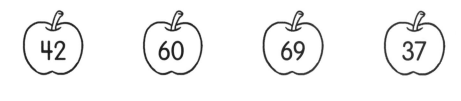

_____, _____, _____, _____

greatest

Name: _____ Date: _____

Complete the pattern.
Draw the shape that comes next. (2 points)

23.  _____

Look at the picture.
Fill in the blank. (2 points)

24.

Joe   Kean   Nicole   John   David

Nicole is _____ from the right.

Write + or – in each circle. (2 × 1 point = 2 points)

25.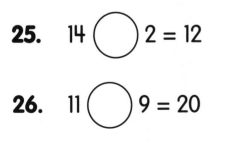

14 ◯ 2 = 12

26. 11 ◯ 9 = 20

Look at the picture.
Fill in the blanks. (2 × 2 points = 4 points)

Each 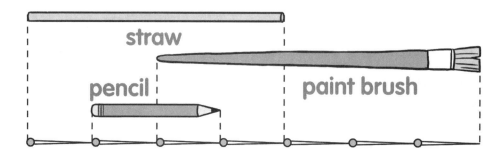 stands for 1 unit.

27. The pencil is about _____ ⊶━━ long.

28. The longest object is the _____.

Fill in the blanks. (2 points)

29.

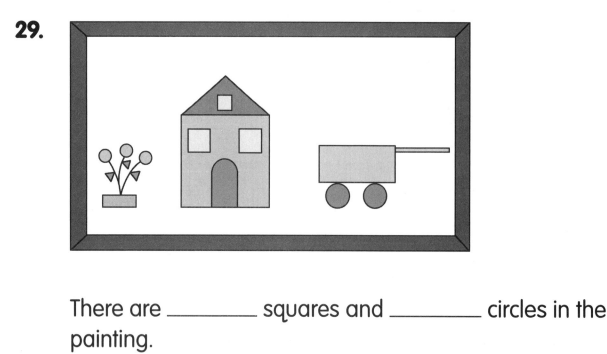

There are _____ squares and _____ circles in the painting.

● **Answer the question.** (2 points)

30.

Which box is lighter? Box _____

Find the missing numbers. (2 points)

31.

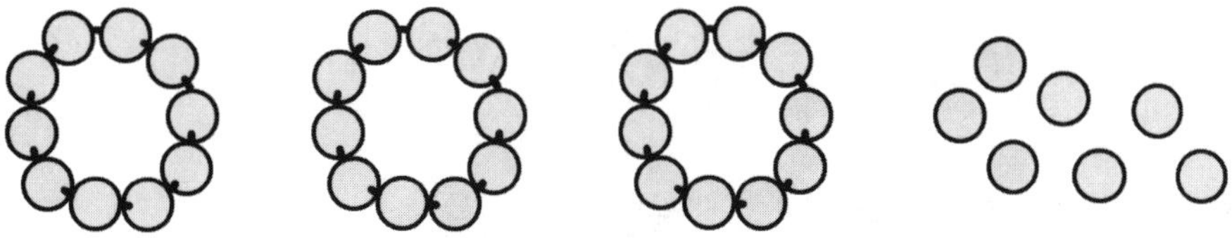

_____ tens _____ ones = _____

Circle.
Then fill in the blank. (2 points)

32.   Put the ladybugs in groups of 4.

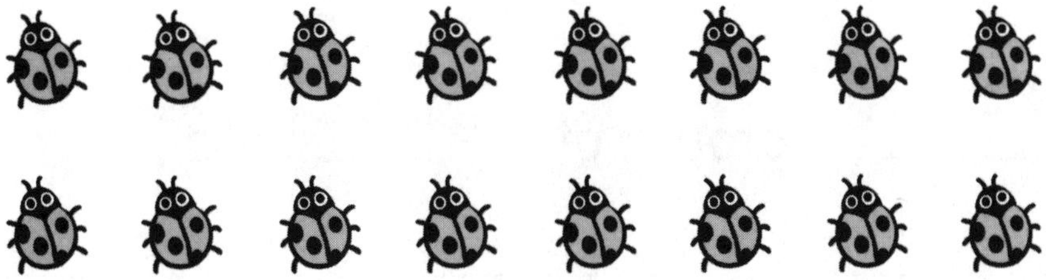

There are _____ groups of 4 ladybugs.

Name: _____ Date: _____

Fill in the blank. (2 points)

33.

3 eights = _____

Circle the answer. (2 points)

34. Which of the following is equal to 69?

54 + 15   61 + 9   40 + 39

Count.
Then fill in the blanks. (4 points)

35.

There are _____ groups of _____ bells.

_____ + _____ + _____ + _____ = _____

36. Complete the number pattern. (2 points)

100, 96, 92, _____, _____, 80, _____

Fill in the blank. (2 points)

37. Take away 3 tens 9 ones from 7 tens 5 ones.

The answer is _____ ones.

38. Circle the two numbers that make 7 tens 16 ones. (1 point)

42   36   44   75   67

39. Circle the two items that cost 58¢ in all. (1 point)

39¢   32¢   19¢   36¢

book   pencil   eraser   notebook

Look at the pictures.
Use them to answer Exercises 40 and 41. (2 × 2 points = 4 points)

1 ○ stands for 1 unit.

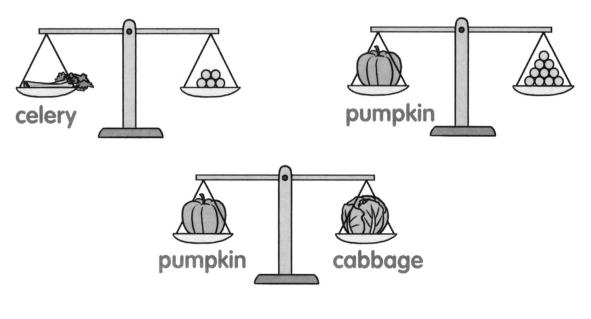

celery

pumpkin

pumpkin   cabbage

40. The weight of the cabbage is about _____ units.

41. The _____ is the lightest.

● Extended Response (5 × 4 points = 20 points)

Solve.
Show your work.
Write the number sentence.

42. There were 8 monkeys in a zoo.
The zookeeper gave 5 bananas to each monkey.
How many bananas did the monkeys get in all?

The monkeys got _____ bananas in all.

43. After buying a box of crayons, Pedro has 27¢ left.
How much did he have at first?

He had _____ at first.

44. Sally has 15 stickers.
She gives 3 stickers to each friend.

   a. How many friends does she give her stickers to?

   She gives her stickers to _____ friends.

   b. If Sally wants to give 4 stickers each to 5 friends, how many stickers does she need in all?

   She needs _____ stickers in all.

45. There are 35 children in the gym.
18 children are girls.

   a. How many children are boys?

_____ children are boys.

   b. 6 more children go into the gym.
How many children are there in all?

There are _____ children in all.

46. Keith has 78 stamps.
Peter has 20 fewer stamps than Keith.

a. How many stamps does Peter have?

Peter has _____ stamps.

b. John has 5 more stamps than Peter.
How many stamps does John have?

John has _____ stamps.

Answers

Chapter 10

Lesson 1

9. heavier than; lighter than
10. heavier than; lighter than
11. as heavy as

12. glass; cup
13. papaya; mango
14. 6; 10; B
15. cow; sheep; chick
16. fish; worm; ant
17. squirrel; mouse; ladybug

Lesson 2

1. 3	2. 2	3. 5
4. 6	5. 5	6. 7
7. 8	8. 10	9. 5
10. 2	11. 3	12. 8
13. 7	14. 11	15. pineapple

Lesson 3

1. 8	2. 6	3. 14
4. 10	5. 3	6. 5
7. cereal	8. cereal	9. 6
10. 8	11. 12	12. 14
13. 16	14. 8	15. 12
16. pineapple		17. watermelon
18. 6		19. 2
20. 4		21. scissors
22. book		23. scissors

24. Accept any of these:
    scissors; pencil case/book
    or pencil case; book

25. 3	26. 6
27. 4	28. 9

29. __D__, __B__, __C__, __A__
    heaviest

Put on Your Thinking Cap!
Thinking Skill: Deduction
Solution:

1. 6	2. 10	3. 3

Thinking Skill: Spatial visualization
Solution:

4. puppy 5. hamster

Lesson 1

1. Ann	2. Kim	3. 8
4. 3	5. 5	6. sun

7. flower 8. 2 9. 3
10. 4 11. 2
12.

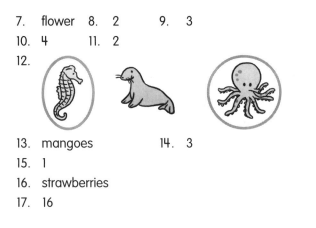

13. mangoes 14. 3
15. 1
16. strawberries
17. 16

Lesson 2
1. 8 2. Jim 3. 2
4. 3 5. 1
6.

Ben's Toys

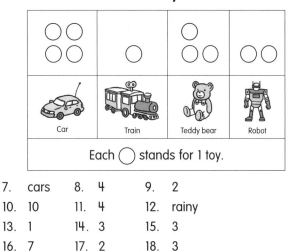

Each ◯ stands for 1 toy.

7. cars 8. 4 9. 2
10. 10 11. 4 12. rainy
13. 1 14. 3 15. 3
16. 7 17. 2 18. 3

Lesson 3
1.

Things	Tally	Number
Frog	IIII	4
Paper boat	III	3
Fish	⊤⊢⊬⌐	5

2. 5 3. 1 4. 9
5.

Items	Tally	Number
Pencil	IIII	4
Notebook	⊤⊢⊬⌐ I	6
Pen	III	3
Sticker	⊤⊢⊬⌐	5

6. notebook 7. 5
8. 3 9. 4
10.

Animals	Tally	Number
Kitten	III	3
Puppy	II	2
Parrot	III	3
Goldfish	IIII	4

11.

Animals in a Pet Shop

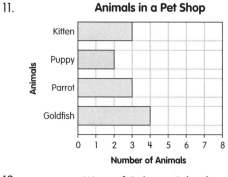

12.

Ways of Going to School

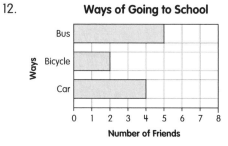

13. 4
14. 3
15. Bus

Put on Your Thinking Cap!
Thinking Skill: Logical reasoning
Solution:
1. rabbit 2. cat
3. 3

Thinking Skill: Spatial visualization
Solution:
4.

Bear Family X	◯ ◯ ◯ ◯
Bear Family Y	◯ ◯ ◯ ◯ ◯ ◯ ◯
Bear Family Z	◯ ◯ ◯ ◯ ◯ ◯
Each ◯ stands for 1 fish.	

5. 18

Chapter 12

Lesson 1

1.

25

2.

27

3.

32

4.

40

5. 24
6. 37
7. 40
8. 28
9. twenty-two
10. thirty
11. twenty-nine
12. thirty-eight
13. thirty-three
14. twenty-five
15. 36
16. 20
17. 7
18. 29
19. 10
20. 20

Lesson 2

1. 2; 3
2. 3; 1
3. 24
4. 37
5. $20 = \underline{2}$ tens $\underline{0}$ ones
   $20 + 0 = \underline{20}$

Tens	Ones
2	0

6. $29 = \underline{2}$ tens $\underline{9}$ ones
   $20 + 9 = \underline{29}$

Tens	Ones
2	9

7. $35 = \underline{3}$ tens $\underline{5}$ ones
   $30 + 5 = \underline{35}$

Tens	Ones
3	5

Lesson 3

1.

25

2.

26

3.

37

4. 26
5. 20
6. 25
7. 34
8. 36
9. 28
10. 33
11. 23
12. 34, 35, $\underline{36}$, 37, $\underline{38}$, 39, $\underline{40}$
13. 22, 24, $\underline{26}$, $\underline{28}$, 30, 32, $\underline{34}$
14. 25, 24, $\underline{23}$, $\underline{22}$, 21, 20, $\underline{19}$
15. 40, 38, 36, $\underline{34}$, $\underline{32}$, 30, $\underline{28}$
16. 40
17. 14
18. 29
19. 38
20. Accept any three of these:
    28; 29; 30; 31; 32; 33; 34
21. Accept any three of these:
    27; 28; 29; 30; 31; 32; 33; 34; 35; 36; 37
22.

23. 29; 23

24. 39; 32

25.
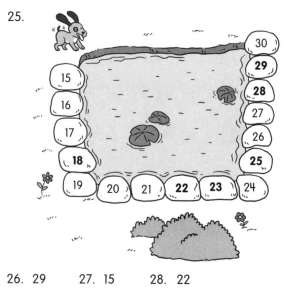

26. 29   27. 15   28. 22

Put on Your Thinking Cap!

1. Thinking Skill: Logical reasoning
   Solution:

5	10	15
10	15	I am the least number 5
I am the greatest number 15	5	10

2. Thinking Skill: Logical reasoning
   Solution:

16	**2**	12
6	10	**14**
8	**18**	4

Chapter 13

Lesson 1

1.

19

2.

37

3. 21 + 5 = 2 tens 1 one + 5 ones
         = 2 tens 6 ones
    (20) (1) = 26

4. 3 + 35 = 3 ones + 3 tens 5 ones
         = 3 tens 8 ones
    (30) (5) = 38

5. 26 + 2 = 2 tens 6 ones + 2 ones
         = 2 tens 8 ones
    (20) (6) = 28

6. 31 + 4 = 3 tens 1 one + 4 ones
         = 3 tens 5 ones
    (30) (1) = 35

7.   Tens Ones
         3   5
      +   4
         3   9

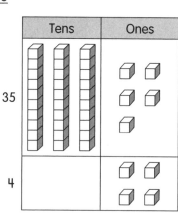

8.
Tens	Ones
2	1
+ 1	6
3	**7**

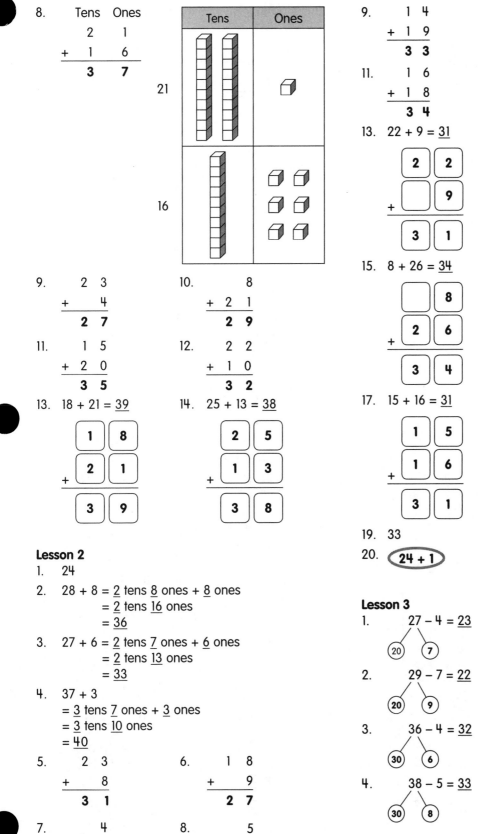

Tens	Ones
21	
16	

9.
```
    2 3
  +   4
    2 7
```

10.
```
      8
  + 2 1
    2 9
```

11.
```
    1 5
  + 2 0
    3 5
```

12.
```
    2 2
  + 1 0
    3 2
```

13. 18 + 21 = <u>39</u>

1	8
+ 2	1
3	**9**

14. 25 + 13 = <u>38</u>

2	5
+ 1	3
3	**8**

Lesson 2

1. 24

2. 28 + 8 = <u>2</u> tens <u>8</u> ones + <u>8</u> ones
       = <u>2</u> tens <u>16</u> ones
       = <u>36</u>

3. 27 + 6 = <u>2</u> tens <u>7</u> ones + <u>6</u> ones
       = <u>2</u> tens <u>13</u> ones
       = <u>33</u>

4. 37 + 3
   = <u>3</u> tens <u>7</u> ones + <u>3</u> ones
   = <u>3</u> tens <u>10</u> ones
   = <u>40</u>

5.
```
    2 3
  +   8
    3 1
```

6.
```
    1 8
  +   9
    2 7
```

7.
```
      4
  + 3 6
    4 0
```

8.
```
      5
  + 2 5
    3 0
```

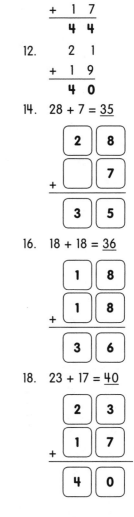

9.
```
    1 4
  + 1 9
    3 3
```

10.
```
    2 7
  + 1 7
    4 4
```

11.
```
    1 6
  + 1 8
    3 4
```

12.
```
    2 1
  + 1 9
    4 0
```

13. 22 + 9 = <u>31</u>

2	2
+	9
3	1

14. 28 + 7 = <u>35</u>

2	8
+	7
3	5

15. 8 + 26 = <u>34</u>

	8
+ 2	6
3	4

16. 18 + 18 = <u>36</u>

1	8
+ 1	8
3	6

17. 15 + 16 = <u>31</u>

1	5
+ 1	6
3	1

18. 23 + 17 = <u>40</u>

2	3
+ 1	7
4	0

19. 33

20. (24 + 1)

21. (29 + 7)

Lesson 3

1. 27 − 4 = <u>23</u>
   (20) (7)

2. 29 − 7 = <u>22</u>
   (20) (9)

3. 36 − 4 = <u>32</u>
   (30) (6)

4. 38 − 5 = <u>33</u>
   (30) (8)

5. $27 - 3 = \underline{2}$ tens $\underline{7}$ ones $- 3$ ones
    $= 2$ tens $\underline{4}$ ones
    $= \underline{24}$

6. $39 - 6 = \underline{3}$ tens 9 ones $- \underline{6}$ ones
    $= \underline{3}$ tens 3 ones
    $= \underline{33}$

7. $35 - 4$
    $= \underline{3}$ tens $\underline{5}$ ones $- \underline{4}$ ones
    $= \underline{3}$ tens $\underline{1}$ one
    $= \underline{31}$

8. 2 tens 8 ones $- 4$ ones $= \underline{28} - \underline{4}$
    $= \underline{24}$

9. 3 tens 7 ones $- 2$ ones $= \underline{37} - \underline{2}$
    $= \underline{35}$

10. 2 tens 6 ones $- 1$ ten 1 one
    $= \underline{26} - \underline{11}$
    $= \underline{15}$

11. | Tens | Ones |
     |------|------|
     | 2 | 8 |
     | − | 6 |
     | **2** | **2** |

12. | Tens | Ones |
     |------|------|
     | 3 | 4 |
     | − | 2 |
     | **3** | **2** |

13. | Tens | Ones |
     |------|------|
     | 3 | 8 |
     | − | 8 |
     | **3** | **0** |

14. | Tens | Ones |
     |------|------|
     | 3 | 7 |
     | − 1 | 5 |
     | **2** | **2** |

15. | Tens | Ones |
     |------|------|
     | 3 | 3 |
     | − 2 | 1 |
     | **1** | **2** |

16. | Tens | Ones |
     |------|------|
     | 2 | 9 |
     | − 1 | 0 |
     | **1** | **9** |

17. $27 - 5 = \underline{22}$

2	7
	5
2	2

18. $39 - 7 = \underline{32}$

3	9
	7
3	2

19. $26 - 15 = \underline{11}$

2	6
1	5
1	1

20. $38 - 12 = \underline{26}$

3	8
1	2
2	6

21. $24 - 14 = \underline{10}$

2	4
1	4
1	0

22. $35 - 30 = \underline{5}$

3	5
3	0
	5

Lesson 4

1.
```
    2 4
  −   6
    1 8
```

2.
```
    2 1
  −   9
    1 2
```

3.
```
    3 0
  −   8
    2 2
```

4.
```
    3 2
  −   5
    2 7
```

5.
```
    2 7
  − 1 8
      9
```

6.
```
    3 3
  − 1 6
    1 7
```

7.
```
    3 5
  − 1 9
    1 6
```

8.
```
    4 0
  − 1 5
    2 5
```

9. $24 - 9 = \underline{15}$

2	4
	9
1	5

10. $36 - 8 = \underline{28}$

3	6
	8
2	8

11. $26 - 17 = \underline{9}$

2	6
1	7
	9

12. $30 - 11 = \underline{19}$

3	0
1	1
1	9

13. $34 - 18 = \underline{16}$

3	4
1	8
1	6

14. $40 - 27 = \underline{13}$

4	0
2	7
1	3

15.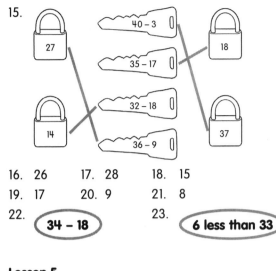

16. 26 17. 28 18. 15
19. 17 20. 9 21. 8
22. **34 – 18** 23. **6 less than 33**

Lesson 5
1. 18 2. 21 3. 17
4. 16 5. 21 6. 19
7. 20
8.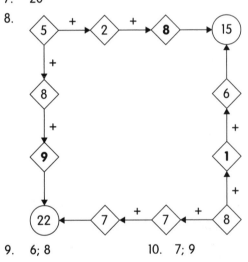

9. 6; 8 10. 7; 9

Lesson 6
1. 20 – 6 = 14
 Serene has <u>14</u> muffins left.
2. 15 + 9 = 24
 David has <u>24</u> stickers in all.
3. 36 – 12 = 24
 Joanne has <u>24</u> marbles left.
4. 27 + 8 = 35
 Eugene has <u>35</u> magnets.

Put on Your Thinking Cap!
1. Thinking Skill: Spatial visualization
 Solution: Answers vary.
 Samples: Add 17, subtract 0.
     Add 18, subtract 1.
     Add 19, subtract 2.

2. Thinking Skill: Comparing
 Strategy: Make a list
 Solution: 28
 He will be <u>28</u> years old in 2012.
3. Thinking Skill: Identifying patterns & relationships
 Strategy: Look for patterns
 Solution:

38	37	36
36	35	**34**
34	33	**32**
32	**31**	**30**

Chapter 14

Lesson 1
1. 11 2. 8 3. 15
4. 18 5. 13 6. 17
7. 17 8. 18 9. 12
10. 17 11. 29 12. 29
13. 17 14. 18 15. 29
16. 26 17. 34 18. 36
19. 39 20. 38 21. 28
22. 36 23. 32 24. 27
25. 35 26. 34 27. 23
28. 26

Lesson 2
1. 5 2. 4 3. 7
4. 8 5. 4 6. 8
7. 23 8. 22 9. 21
10. 24 11. 33 12. 31
13. 31 14. 34 15. 11
16. 18 17. 14 18. 25
19. 22 20. 4 21. 9
22. 17 23. 13 24. 5
25. 9 26. 1

Put on Your Thinking Cap!

1. Thinking Skill: Identifying patterns &
    relationships
    Strategy: Look for patterns
    Solution:

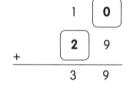

2. Thinking Skill: Identifying patterns &
    relationships
    Strategy: Look for patterns
    Solution:

Thinking Skill: Deduction
Strategy: Work backward
Solution:

3.
```
  1  [0]
   [2]  9
+
  3  9
```

4.
```
  [1]  9
   1  [9]
+
  3  8
```

Chapter 15

Lesson 1

1. 7   2. Sunday
3. August 4, 2009   4. August 13, 2009
5. Monday   6. 31
7. summer   8. 31
9. Friday   10. Wednesday
11. 5   12. December 6, 2009
13. December 25, 2009   14. January
15. winter

Lesson 2

1. 5   2. 1   3. 3
4. 11   5. 7   6. 2
7. 7 o'clock   8. 8 o'clock
9. 10 o'clock   10. 6 o'clock

Lesson 3

1.
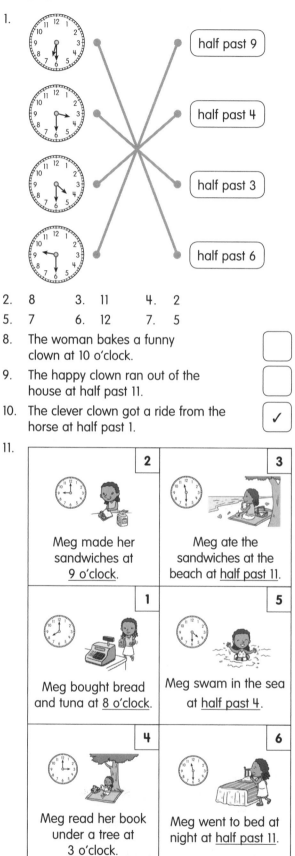

half past 9
half past 4
half past 3
half past 6

2. 8   3. 11   4. 2
5. 7   6. 12   7. 5

8. The woman bakes a funny
    clown at 10 o'clock.   ☐

9. The happy clown ran out of the
    house at half past 11.   ☐

10. The clever clown got a ride from the
    horse at half past 1.   ✓

11.

	2		3
Meg made her sandwiches at <u>9 o'clock</u>.		Meg ate the sandwiches at the beach at <u>half past 11</u>.	

	1		5
Meg bought bread and tuna at <u>8 o'clock</u>.		Meg swam in the sea at <u>half past 4</u>.	

	4		6
Meg read her book under a tree at <u>3 o'clock</u>.		Meg went to bed at night at <u>half past 11</u>.	

Put on Your Thinking Cap!

1. Thinking Skill: Sequencing
   Strategy: Make a systematic list
   Solution: 11; 11

2. Strategy: Guess and check
   Solution:

Test Prep for Chapters 10 to 15

1. C   2. C   3. B
4. B   5. A   6. C
7. D   8. A   9. B
10. A
11. 13   12. 6
13. 27
14. twenty-seven   15. Wednesday
16. Monday   17. 5
18. 7   19. 24
20. <u>19</u>, <u>21</u>, <u>25</u>, <u>34</u>
    least
21. 36, 33, 30, <u>27</u>, <u>24</u>, 21
22. half past 4
23. <u>32</u> – <u>14</u> = <u>18</u>
24. ☀ = 15

    ☾ = 10
25. 4   26. spring
27. October; fall   28. Monday
29. 24 – 9 = 15
    <u>15</u> muffins are left.
30. 18 + 22 = 40
    Jessica counts <u>40</u> flowers
    in all.

Chapter 16

Lesson 1

1. 3
2. <u>4</u> tens = <u>40</u> = <u>forty</u>
3. 10, … <u>20</u>, … <u>30</u>, 31, 32, <u>33</u>, <u>34</u>, 35
4. 10, … 20, … <u>30</u>, … <u>40</u>, … <u>50</u>, … <u>60</u>,
   70, … <u>80</u>, … <u>90</u>, <u>91</u>, <u>92</u> 93, 94, <u>95</u>,
   <u>96</u>, <u>97</u>, <u>98</u>

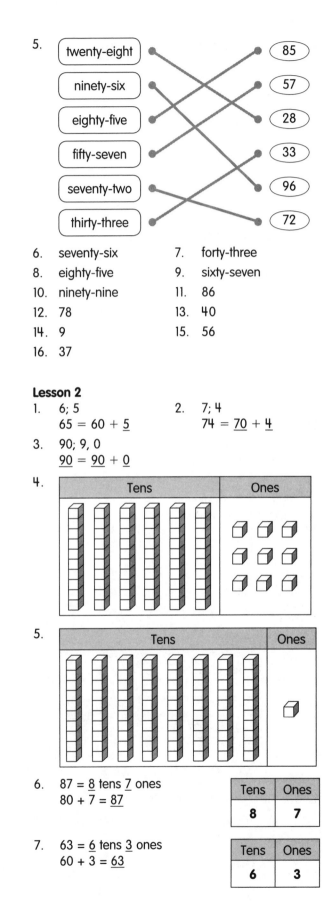

5.
twenty-eight	→	85
ninety-six	→	57
eighty-five	→	28
fifty-seven	→	33
seventy-two	→	96
thirty-three	→	72

6. seventy-six   7. forty-three
8. eighty-five   9. sixty-seven
10. ninety-nine   11. 86
12. 78   13. 40
14. 9   15. 56
16. 37

Lesson 2

1. 6; 5   2. 7; 4
   65 = 60 + <u>5</u>   74 = <u>70</u> + <u>4</u>
3. 90; 9, 0
   <u>90</u> = <u>90</u> + <u>0</u>

4.
Tens	Ones

5.
Tens	Ones

6. 87 = <u>8</u> tens <u>7</u> ones
   80 + 7 = <u>87</u>

Tens	Ones
8	7

7. 63 = <u>6</u> tens <u>3</u> ones
   60 + 3 = <u>63</u>

Tens	Ones
6	3

8. 92 = <u>9</u> tens <u>2</u> ones
90 + 2 = <u>92</u>

Tens	Ones
9	2

Lesson 3

1. 59   2. 65   3. 83
4. 65   5. 76   6. 82
7. 96   8. 56   9. 61
10. 76   11. 98   12. 100
13. 49
14. 49; 62
15. 93; 100
16. 62
17. <u>82</u> , <u>70</u> , <u>47</u> , <u>32</u>
    greatest
18. 30, <u>40</u>, <u>50</u>, 60, 70
19. 42, 44, <u>46</u>, 48, <u>50</u>, <u>52</u>
20. 74, 72, <u>70</u>, <u>68</u>, 66, <u>64</u>
21. 80, <u>75</u>, 70, <u>65</u>, <u>60</u>, 55

Put on Your Thinking Cap!

1. Thinking Skill: Deduction
    Strategy: Solve part of the problem
    Solution: Sam: 8; Brian: 14; Shawn: 8; 30

Thinking Skill: Deduction
Strategy: Make a list
Solution:

2. 44   3. 68

Chapter 17

Lesson 1

1. 65 + 4 = <u>69</u>

    65, 66, <u>67</u>, <u>68</u>, <u>69</u>

2. 53 + 5 = <u>58</u>

    53, <u>54</u>, <u>55</u>, <u>56</u>, <u>57</u>, <u>58</u>

3.   7 3   4.   5
     +   6   +   6 2
        7 9   6 7

5.   4 0   6.   3 5
     + 2 5   + 5 3
        6 5   8 8

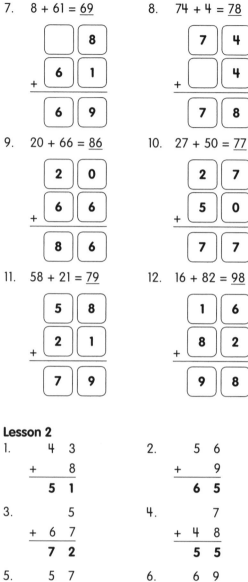

7. 8 + 61 = <u>69</u>   8. 74 + 4 = <u>78</u>

9. 20 + 66 = <u>86</u>   10. 27 + 50 = <u>77</u>

11. 58 + 21 = <u>79</u>   12. 16 + 82 = <u>98</u>

Lesson 2

1.   4 3   2.   5 6
     +   8   +   9
        5 1   6 5

3.   5   4.   7
     + 6 7   + 4 8
        7 2   5 5

5.   5 7   6.   6 9
     + 3 3   + 2 4
        9 0   9 3

7.   4 3   8.   8 5
     + 4 8   + 1 5
        9 1   1 0 0

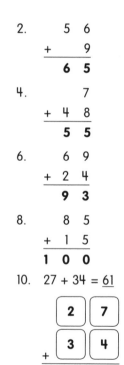

9. 64 + 16 = <u>80</u>   10. 27 + 34 = <u>61</u>

11. $48 + 35 = \underline{83}$

4	8
+ 3	5
8	3

12. $26 + 55 = \underline{81}$

2	6
+ 5	5
8	1

13. $51 + 29 = \underline{80}$

5	1
+ 2	9
8	0

14. $77 + 17 = \underline{94}$

7	7
+ 1	7
9	4

15.

48 + 35		71
88 + 12		93
67 + 26		83
13 + 58		100
37 + 15		81
42 + 28		52
64 + 17		70

16. 82
17. 41
18. 63
19. 72
20. 83
21. 91
22. 100
23. 94

I CAN DO IT!

Lesson 3

1.
```
  5 7
-   4
  5 3
```

2.
```
  8 8
-   6
  8 2
```

3.
```
  9 9
- 7 0
  2 9
```

4.
```
  6 5
- 3 3
  3 2
```

5. $45 - 3 = \underline{42}$

4	5
−	3
4	2

6. $79 - 8 = \underline{71}$

7	9
−	8
7	1

7. $68 - 50 = \underline{18}$

6	8
− 5	0
1	8

8. $86 - 22 = \underline{64}$

8	6
− 2	2
6	4

9.

86 − 6		4 tens 5 ones
49 − 4		8 tens
88 − 3		5 tens 2 ones
57 − 5		8 tens 5 ones

10.

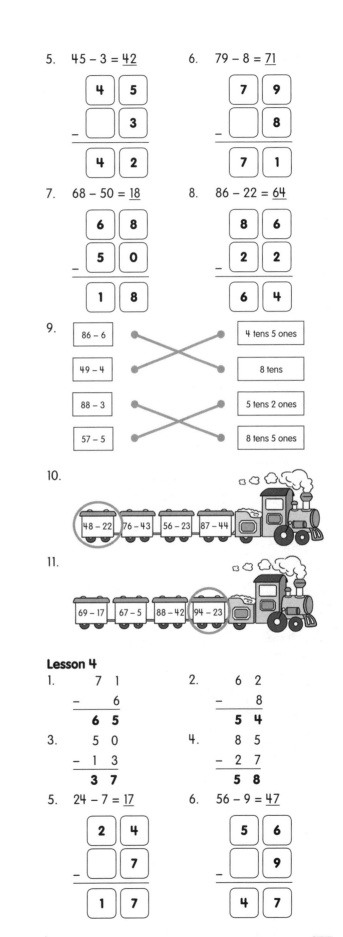

48 − 22   76 − 43   56 − 23   87 − 44

11.

69 − 17   67 − 5   88 − 42   94 − 23

Lesson 4

1.
```
  7 1
-   6
  6 5
```

2.
```
  6 2
-   8
  5 4
```

3.
```
  5 0
- 1 3
  3 7
```

4.
```
  8 5
- 2 7
  5 8
```

5. $24 - 7 = \underline{17}$

2	4
−	7
1	7

6. $56 - 9 = \underline{47}$

5	6
−	9
4	7

7. $80 - 45 = \underline{35}$

$$\begin{array}{cc} \boxed{8} & \boxed{0} \\ -\ \boxed{4} & \boxed{5} \\ \hline \boxed{3} & \boxed{5} \end{array}$$

8. $71 - 28 = \underline{43}$

$$\begin{array}{cc} \boxed{7} & \boxed{1} \\ -\ \boxed{2} & \boxed{8} \\ \hline \boxed{4} & \boxed{3} \end{array}$$

9.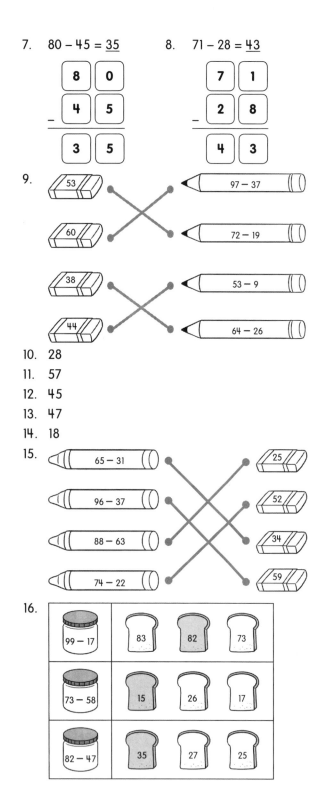

10. 28

11. 57

12. 45

13. 47

14. 18

15.

16.

17.

© 2009 Marshall Cavendish International (Singapore) Private Limited. Copying is permitted; see page ii.

Put on Your Thinking Cap!
Thinking Skill: Deduction
Strategy: Solve part of the problem
Solution:

1. 35   2. 44   3. 67
4. 9   5. 32   6. 23

Thinking Skill: Deduction
Strategy: Work backward

7. 34   8. 68

Lesson 1

1. $\underline{2} + \underline{2} + \underline{2} + \underline{2} = \underline{8}$
   $\underline{4}$ twos = $\underline{8}$
   There are $\underline{8}$ frogs in all.

2.

20; 20

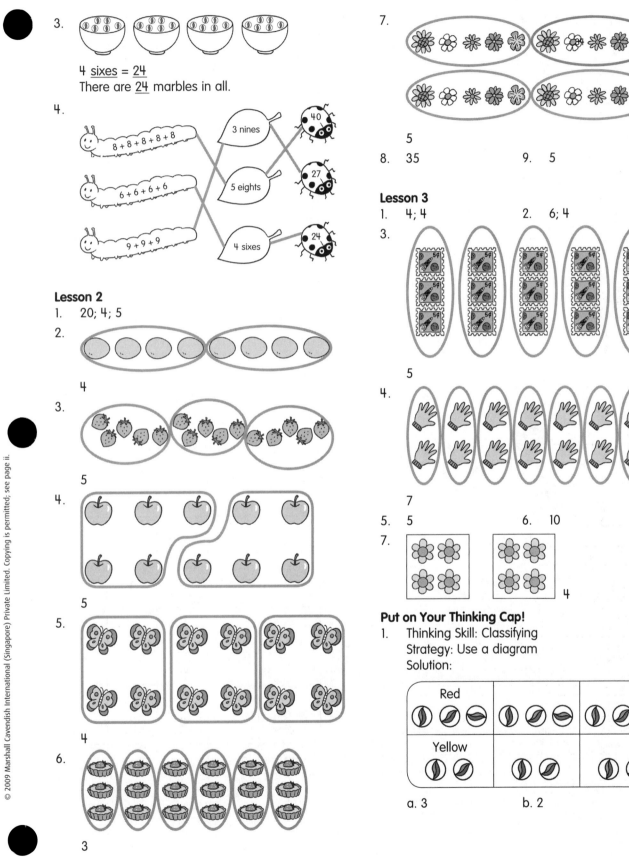

3.

4 sixes = 24
There are 24 marbles in all.

4.

Lesson 2

1. 20; 4; 5

2.

4

3.

5

4.

5

5.

4

6.

3

7.

5

8. 35   9. 5

Lesson 3

1. 4; 4   2. 6; 4

3.

5

4.

7

5. 5   6. 10

7.

4

Put on Your Thinking Cap!

1. Thinking Skill: Classifying
   Strategy: Use a diagram
   Solution:

   a. 3   b. 2

2. Thinking Skill: Comparing
   Strategy: Use a diagram
   Solution:

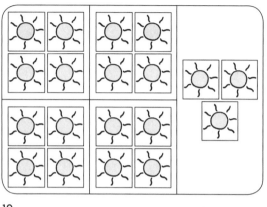

19

Lesson 1

1.

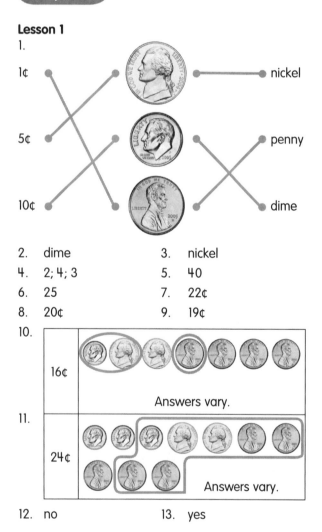

1¢   nickel

5¢   penny

10¢   dime

2. dime	3. nickel
4. 2; 4; 3	5. 40
6. 25	7. 22¢
8. 20¢	9. 19¢

10.

16¢	Answers vary.

11.

24¢	Answers vary.

12. no   13. yes

Lesson 2

1. 5   2. 10

3.   ✓

   ☐

   ✓

4. Answers vary.
5. Answers vary.
6. Answers vary.
7. Answers vary.
8. Answers vary.

Lesson 3

1. 70¢   2. 30¢
3. 65¢   4. 89¢
5. 50¢

6.   ☐

   ✓

7.

	quarter	dime	nickel	penny
Using 4 coins	4			
Using 6 coins	3	2	1	
Using 7 coins	2	5		
Using 10 coins		10		
Using 12 coins		8	4	
Using 100 coins				100

8.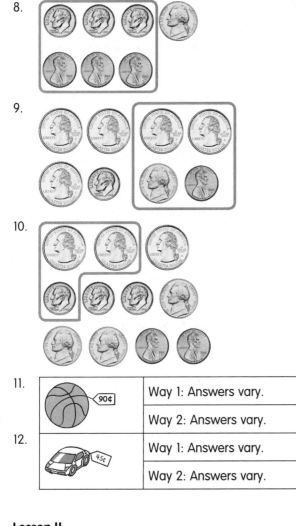

9.

10.

11.

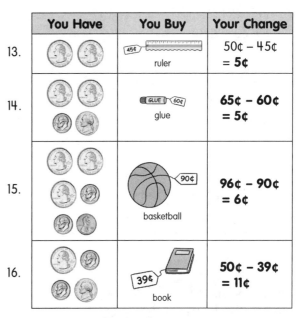 basketball 90¢	Way 1: Answers vary.
	Way 2: Answers vary.

12.

car 45¢	Way 1: Answers vary.
	Way 2: Answers vary.

	You Have	You Buy	Your Change
13.		ruler 45¢	50¢ – 45¢ = 5¢
14.		glue 60¢	**65¢ – 60¢ = 5¢**
15.		basketball 90¢	**96¢ – 90¢ = 6¢**
16.		book 39¢	**50¢ – 39¢ = 11¢**

17. 50¢ – 25¢ – 15¢ = 10¢
She has <u>10¢</u> left.

18. 5¢ + 30¢ + 8¢ = 43¢
He spends <u>43¢</u> in all.

19. 40¢ – 15¢ = 25¢
Carmen pays <u>25¢</u> more than Gomez.

20. 15¢ + 13¢ = 28¢
He had <u>28¢</u> at first.

Put on Your Thinking Cap!
Thinking Skill: Comparing
Strategy: Guess and check
Solution:

1. Robot; building blocks

2. Checkers set; yo-yo

3. Thinking Skill: Deduction
Strategy: Use a diagram
Solution:

Sarah	Amy	Neil	Pedro
<u>89¢</u>	<u>95¢</u>	<u>70¢</u>	<u>90¢</u>

End-of-Year Test Prep

1. D   2. B   3. B
4. D   5. D   6. B
7. D   8. A   9. B
10. A   11. D   12. B
13. B   14. C   15. D
16. B   17. B   18. A
19. D   20. A

Lesson 4

1. 65
2. <u>50¢ + 35¢ = 85¢</u>
3. <u>40¢ + 30¢ = 70¢</u>
4. <u>20¢ + 10¢ = 30¢</u>
She spends <u>30¢</u>.
5. <u>40¢ + 15¢ = 55¢</u>
He spends <u>55¢</u>.
6. <u>20¢ + 10¢ = 30¢</u>
He spends <u>30¢</u>.
7.
tube 20¢   bell 30¢   cap 85¢
yogurt 40¢   muffin 60¢
8. 65¢
9. 22¢
10. 22¢
11. <u>75¢ – 60¢ = 15¢</u>
12. <u>60¢ – 30¢ = 30¢</u>

21. forty-eight

22. <u>69</u>, <u>60</u>, <u>42</u>, <u>37</u>
    greatest

23.

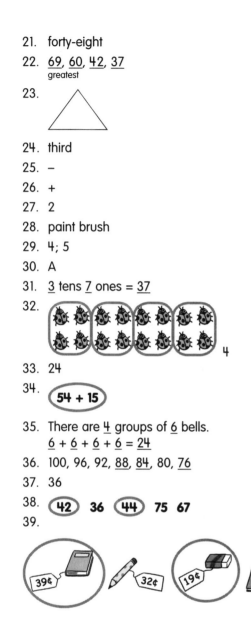

24. third

25. −

26. +

27. 2

28. paint brush

29. 4; 5

30. A

31. <u>3</u> tens <u>7</u> ones = <u>37</u>

32. 4

33. 24

34. $54 + 15$

35. There are <u>4</u> groups of <u>6</u> bells.
    <u>6</u> + <u>6</u> + <u>6</u> + <u>6</u> = <u>24</u>

36. 100, 96, 92, <u>88</u>, <u>84</u>, 80, <u>76</u>

37. 36

38. (42) 36 (44) 75 67

39.

40. 10

41. celery

42. 5 + 5 + 5 + 5 + 5 + 5 + 5 + 5 = 40
    The monkeys got <u>40</u> bananas in all.

43. 27¢ + 65¢ = 92¢
    He had <u>92</u>¢ at first.

44. a.

   She gives her stickers to
   <u>5</u> friends.
   b. 4 + 4 + 4 + 4 + 4 = 20
   She needs <u>20</u> stickers in all.

45. a. 35 − 18 = 17
    <u>17</u> children are boys.
    b. 35 + 6 = 41
    There are <u>41</u> children in all.

46. a. 78 − 20 = 58
    Peter has <u>58</u> stamps.
    b. 58 + 5 = 63
    John has <u>63</u> stamps.

BLANK

BLANK